O N
F O O T

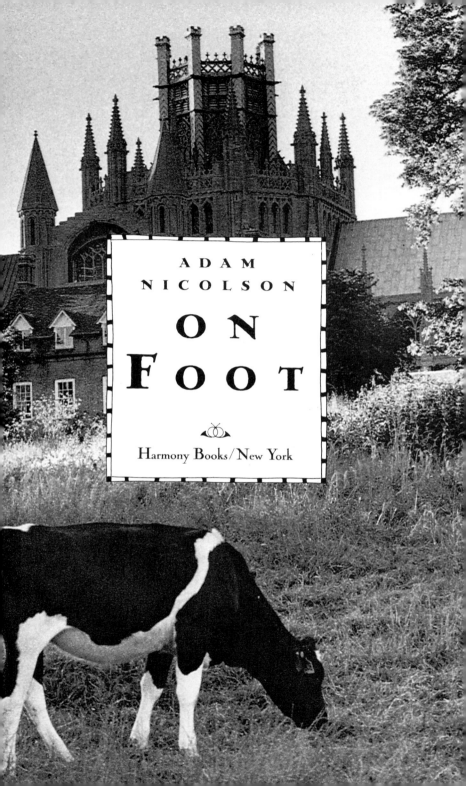

ADAM
NICOLSON

ON
FOOT

Harmony Books / New York

P. *1 After lunch – outside Gatcombe Church on the Isle of Wight.*

PP. *2–3 Ely Cathedral and the meadows to the south of it.*

ENDPAPERS *The Sound of Taransay, Harris.*

Published by Harmony Books, New York, New York 10022, 201 East 50th Street. Member of the Crown Publishing Group. Originally published in Great Britain by George Weidenfeld & Nicolson Ltd. HARMONY and colophon are trademarks of Crown Publishers, Inc.

Manufactured in Great Britain

Library of Congress Cataloguing-in-Publication Data
Nicolson, Adam 1957–
On foot: guided walks in England, France and the U.S./ Adam Nicolson.
    p.   cm.
    1. Walking—Great Britain—Guide-books. 2. Walking—France—Guide-books. 3. Walking—United States—Guide-books. 4. Great Britain—Description and travel—1981—   —Guide-books. 5. France—Description and travel—1981—   —Guide-books. 6. United States—Description and travel—1981—   —Guide-books. I. Title.
796.5'1—dc20
                                        90-4963
                                        CIP

ISBN 0-517-58174-4
10 9 8 7 6 5 4 3 2 1
First American Edition

Author's Acknowledgments

I have many people to thank: above all my editors at the *Sunday Times* – Dick Girling, Will Ellsworth-Jones and Christine Sykes, all of whom have been highly tolerant of every conceivable waywardness; at Weidenfeld – Michael Dover, Colin Grant, Barbara Mellor and Coralie Hepburn; and my friends and family who came with me on some of these walks – David and Kanthi Barry, Simon Craven, Montagu and Sarah Don, Deborah Karl, Mark Katzenellenbogen, Hugh MacSween, Jeremy Newick, Nigel, Olivia, Rebecca, Thomas and William Nicolson, Sarah Raven, Stephen Romer, Robert Sackville West, Bridget Strevens, Doug Stumpf, Christopher Twigg, Charlie Waite, Cecily West, and Peter and Esther Zinovieff. It would not have been half as much fun without them.

Design and maps by Rita Wüthrich

Picture Acknowledgments

All photographs were taken by Philip Dunn except the following:
    Mike Wilkinson endpapers, 45, 47, 95, 97
    Patrick Sutherland 2–3, 86, 87, 88
    Janine Wiedel 23, 25, 67, 68, 69
    Adam Nicolson 50, 53, 54, 115, 116, 118, 119
    Oliver Rackham 65 (above)
    A. F. Kersting 73, 74, 75
    Mike Booher 81
    U.S. National Park Service 82
    Carl Glassman 90, 91, 92
    Office Départemental du Tourisme de la Manche 108, 110
    French Government Tourist Office 109

Contents

Introduction

'Have you any business with me, Sir Willful?' the exquisitely urban and alarmingly beautiful Millamant, heroine of Congreve's *Way of the World*, asks her lumpen cousin. He's up from the country, desperate for her, too gawky to get his words out straight.
    SIR WILLFUL: Not at present cousin. – Yes, I made bold to see, to come and know if that how you were disposed to fetch a walk this evening....
    MILLAMANT: A walk? What then?
    SIR WILLFUL: Nay, nothing – only for the walk's sake, that's all –
    MILLAMANT: I nauseate walking; 'tis a country diversion; I loathe the country and everything that relates to it.
    Being Sir Willful for a while is a burden that every walker must carry. It's not an elegant or a metropolitan thing to be doing with one's time. It is, in a way, a casting loose from all those things, an abandonment of sophistication, a simple reversion to the state, as one seventeenth-century walker was described, in which 'He used his ten toes for a nagge' and where the only qualifications for success are 'good WIND and great BOTTOM.'
    A walk is all about wind and bottom. It is not a good place either to think or talk. In an essay on walking, with which he had little sympathy, Max Beerbohm decided that nothing rots the mind faster than going for a walk. Someone who the evening before had been the quickest, most allusive of dinner companions, casually moving from medieval cosmology to the nature of love, his mind playing with ease over the surface of life, was reduced on a walk to reading signs. 'Bed *and* Breakfast,' he says after a mile or so; '*Strictly* private' follows an hour later, and the urban sophisticate tags along mopingly behind, desperate for the drawing-room where wit and precision might return.
    No, the pleasures of walking are not really civilized; they are outside the understanding of anyone really engaged in the workings of the civilized world. There is one critical moment in the history of

6

Wasdale Head, Cumbria, with Scott Naylor, the owner of the farmhouse which was Adam Nicolson's base for a wintertime walk in the Lake District (see pp. 152–8).

walking when this gap – between the way walkers understand the world and the way everyone else does – becomes all too apparent. When Coleridge was staying with the Wordsworths in the Quantocks in 1797–8, going for moonlit walks together among the hills and along the rivers, slowly formulating the tone and theme of the *Lyrical Ballads*, they were being secretly tailed by a Home Office spy. The spy couldn't quite make out what the poets were doing. He knew they were Jacobin revolutionaries but what was this? Were they investigating possible landing spots and future strongholds for an invasion from France? Was their inerest in moonlit rivers a reconnaissance to do with navigability? Why at night-time? What was so secret about this obsessive, repetitive wandering around a small bit of Somerset? What were they trying to find out? He never knew. How could he?

The two poets embody the two ways of walking; I veer between them. Wordsworth-walking is solid, continuous and consistently rhythmical. The walk is the thing more than what is walked over. The walk in this book along the great beach of Hatteras Island, forty miles of consistent beach, is in classic Wordsworth style, unbroken, never jumpy, moving steadily and smoothly over a level surface for hour after hour and mile after mile, so that all that matters in the

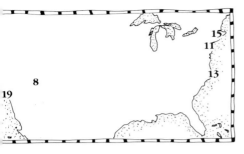

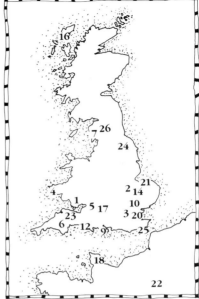

Maps of the USA and Britain with northern France, showing the location of the walks featured in this book. The numbers refer to the relevant chapters, where a more detailed route map for the walk is given.

end is the moving of your legs and the scuffing of your boots on the sand. It's a steady and mindless state. Wordsworth used to hug rocks and trees after too much of this, to reassure himself that something was fixed. (That's one great change in the history of the world: Dr Johnson kicked rocks to demonstrate to others how real things were; Wordsworth hugged them to convince himself of his own reality.)

Coleridge-walking could not be more different. Wordsworth loved road-walking, seeing the road climbing continuous ahead of him up the hill, but Coleridge loved brushing through difficulty, fending off the branches of a thicket as he struggled through it, jump-jerking down pathless hillsides, like a skier in the moguls, reacting, bouncing between crags, ending up in appallingly dangerous, unthought-about corners, from which he somehow escaped. When he found himself on a normal path, as Hazlitt noticed on a walking tour with him, he couldn't keep to a straight line, but wandered to and fro across the line, ambling shambolically towards his destination like a man who didn't know where it was, covering huge distances one minute, hardly moving the next, talking the whole time, either to himself, or into his notebook, or to anyone who happened to be there to listen, a maze of a man, invaded, gripped by, grappling with everything there was to handle or imagine.

There's no need to be a devotee of one or other of these styles.

Both have their pleasures, both respond to different elements in the world, both are a form of freedom – Wordsworth's from attending to anything that is happening except within himself; Coleridge's from any impediment to the way his mind and body can wander. These are the two halves of the romantic spirit – the freedom of the self indulged and the freedom that comes from abandoning yourself to all the insistent realities of the world seen from your own two feet. The good walk is a combination of both halves, in which the state of mind is a strange and paradoxical one – a sort of generous-hearted selfishness, an insistence on doing what has to be done, but an openness to what's going on around you, a valuing of both the journey and the arrival. When a walk is like that, nothing on earth is better.

The walks collected in this book were done in the space of a little over two years, appearing once a month in the London *Sunday Times*. As a collection, there is little that is coherent about it; the walks wander here and there between large cities and deserted places, through villages and small towns, industrial landscapes and undilutedly rural ones. But this is as it should be, as a walk is taking what comes, seeing what surprise is around the next corner; the walks are nothing more than the trace of my interests or curiosities over a series of months. If one thing does connect them, it is that walking can happen anywhere – between Soho bars, in the Utah desert, on midwinter mountains, among the rich men's flowering lawns of southern California. Walking is not like a round of dressage. There is no need to get oneself over-geared up for it. It is the very opposite of that. I once read a book about walking in Sardinia which contained a single piece of advice: young women should not venture into the mountains alone. Here is this book's equivalent: make sure you don't always know exactly what you're doing.

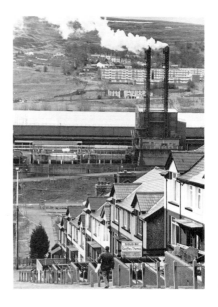

Ebbw Vale, Wales, and the British Steel plant (see pp. 10–15).

9

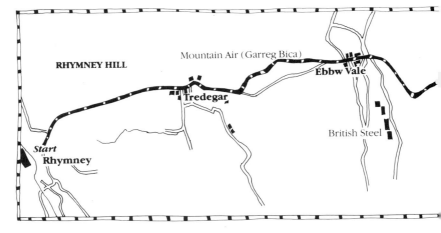

I.

Across Ridge and Valley

Rhymney to Blaenavon

SOUTH WALES

The small village of Rhymney is almost at the head of a narrow mining valley in South Wales. You can have no doubt when you are there that it is a poor place: a perfectly habitable, if unimproved, two-bedroom house will cost £6,000; the village street has the look of a hand with its nails chewed. The man in the estate agent's office told me I came from a different world, choosing his words carefully, a 'more *independent* world'. For there is a repeated insistence here, from almost everyone you meet, on that over-used and sentimentalized word: community. The suspicion arises, as you follow this day's walk across four of the ridges that separate the most famous of the South Wales valleys, that community is what people must turn to when they have little else.

You get the picture in the S & G café in Rhymney village street. Have a cup of coffee there. It is mugged-up at this time of year, with condensation on the windows, a slightly chipped and bruised air to the place and endless teasing banter between the young men. In the valleys to the east, Rhymney has the reputation of being the haunt of some fairly wild boys, outdone only by their neighbours in

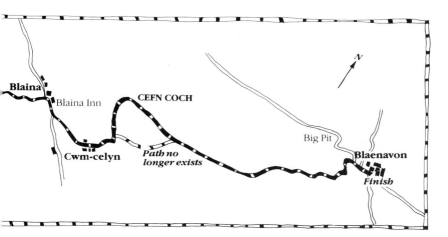

Pontlottyn to the south. So here it is straightaway: poverty and community, the two complementaries on which these intense and concentrated valleys are based.

Of course, there is far more to it. Above all, there is the astonishing layering of each valley. As you climb up away from the road on to Rhymney Hill (called, like every other ridge here, 'the mountain'), you make an instant transition from the industrial world of the valley to the entirely pre-industrial world of the hill. You leave behind the cinder-grit of the village – spattered like all the others with chapels – for the damp, sheep-grazed moor, where the patched-up, corrugated mess of independence that is the typical hill-farm overlooks the neat packages of renewed urban housing below. The change happens within a matter of yards. There is nothing suburban or transitional.

And then as you climb higher, leaving the farm behind in its turn, with the west wind at this time of year blowing you on and up in the most exhilarating of ways, you find yourself on a plateau which appears to stretch almost indefinitely and uninterruptedly in front of you, with the fringes of the moor grasses just emerging from the snow and, everywhere around you, the beautiful harshness of a world removed from human beings.

For the people living and working in the valleys, this instantly available other world has always made the conditions of life more tolerable. As I walked from ridge to ridge and valley to valley, I met a series of people who spoke about the times they had had on the mountain: a woman in the laundrette in Tredegar used to take the bus out to the Beaufort Ballrooms, just north of Ebbw Vale ('it's all bingo halls now'), and then walk back over the top, with a boy, at night. A woman in Ebbw Vale itself remembered the lights of the miners coming back down the hill from Blaina on their way home at the end of a shift, and how men had got lost in blizzards and froze to death – even on the paths they usually took home from work. Then there was a man in Blaina, who had fallen eighty feet from the top of the winding gear at Beynon's Colliery in that valley, and whose face was veined blue from the impact and each of whose arms was now fixed in a constant and unstretchable 'V' (he joked with his still movable right wrist that this position was nevertheless OK for drinking). He told me how, when he was a boy or a young man in the 1920s, when there was little work 'and there was no telly then', he used to go up adventuring with friends on the ridge to the east of Blaina, the Mynydd James, and never better than on a moonlit night when you could see as well as during the day. To walk from there as far as the view over Blaenavon itself was a Sunday outing for all miners' families in the summer.

In this way, despite the first impressions, the world of the ridge was always absorbed and made use of by the valley. As you come over the top of Rhymney Hill and then down towards Tredegar, there, symbolically, over to your right and just encroaching on the mountain edge, are the tombstones of yet another cemetery.

But the double world of mountain and mine has almost come to an end now. The landscape is a litany of closure: the last Tredegar pit, Ty-Trist, in 1959; the last Blaina pit, Beynon's, in 1975; the last at Blaenavon, Big Pit (now a tourist attraction), in April 1980.

A great deal of the industrial rawness has gone, the slag heaps smoothed out in giant cosmetic surgery, the pit-head gear tidied away by scrap merchants. But the roughness has been transferred to the towns themselves. In Tredegar, gutters have rotted and now spit all over the pavement with the melting snow. The Greyhound Hotel in the centre of the town is a gap-toothed wreck. Marginal businesses display temporary signs. The names of terraces you pass as you climb up the far side – Edward, Victoria, York, Kimberley – can only taunt with the memories of another age.

And then, again, you are out of it in an instant, and back into agricultural Wales. The farm on the ridge between Tredegar and Ebbw Vale is called Mountain Air on the map. 'Never heard of that,' a man marking his sheep on the far side of Ebbw Vale told me. 'It's called Garreg Bica.' The forty-acre farm split between two brothers, is up for sale. The original asking price (kite-flying, of course) of £120,000 has been halved, still with no takers.

And then on down, in this extraordinary switchback world, to

In the layered landscape of South Wales the housing occupies the middle ground, with the works in the valley below them and the moors above.

Ebbw Vale town centre, gruesomely pedestrianized, with giant flowerpots resembling Hitler's bunker in Berlin and dominated by the palatial trio of the multi-storey car park, Tesco and Kwiksave. Nowhere is there even a hint of the Next, Principles or Storehouse approach to the high street. Slickness is simply absent.

Now comes what is undoubtedly the industrial highpoint of the walk: the British Steel plant at Ebbw Vale. Its vast blue sheds, more than a mile long, occupy almost the entire floor of the valley. At the far southern end, chimneys smoke against the sunlight. Lorries manoeuvre insignificantly around its edges. Scarcely a person is to be seen. It is the most dramatic industrial landscape in Britain: for its hugeness in such a contained site; for the way in which the town of Ebbw Vale appears so neatly subsidiary to it, almost in the medieval way of a town gathered around the skirts of the castle; and for its uncompromising blueness in the crease (when I was there) of a snowy Welsh valley.

Two ridges still separate you from the end of the walk at Blaenavon. The Ordnance Survey tantalisingly marks a pub on the hillside above the steelworks, perfectly positioned for lunch. All I found there was a farm, the usual collection of rusty corrugated iron, a coffee-coloured goat which nibbled me, and a sign saying 'Morning

Mary Davies, who farms at Cwm-celyn and who vigilantly warns any one straying from the right path across her land not to do so.

Star closed permanently'. Up over the ridge to Blaina (not too hard-going, thick in blown snow) and then down hopefully to the Cog and Petal. (Do not miss, by the way, the wonderful Berea Chapel in Blaina, particularly the vast steel discs that hold it together.)

It was at this point I was arrested. *The map is wrong,* or at least out of date. It shows a path going due east of Cwm-celyn, which does not now exist and has been blocked by a Forestry Commission plantation. I nevertheless waded through the plantation along its supposed line, emerged at the top, felt rather pleased with myself and set off for the crest of the ridge, only to hear an enormous shout from about half a mile below me.

I reluctantly went back down to talk to the lady who had produced it. She is the farmer in this little side valley above Blaina. We discussed the difference between the common ground (above her top fence) and private ground (below it), her sheep (they were wintering well), her garden (it won the Blaina design prize) and the stupidities of mapmakers, Englishmen and walkers. She was very nice. I would hate to think of anyone not following the route she then recommended me, which is marked on our map.

At this end of the walk, things polarize. For the next two miles, crossing the broad-backed upland of Cefn Coch, you might as well

Ken Jones rests above the now defunct Big Pit at Blaenavon, where he worked for 46 of his 64 years.

be in the Brecon Beacons – although this is better because nobody else is here. There is not a hint of industry within a hundred miles. Not, that is, until you reach the lip of the mountain that overlooks the Blaenavon valley. Here again, in that sudden transition so characteristic of this part of Wales, you find yourself poised between two worlds. Behind, the uninterrupted tundra of Lapland; in front, the used wreck of a dug-over slice of Montana, the minerals taken out, the landscape looking, as Auden said of Iceland, like the remains of a party nobody had bothered to clear up.

But then again, inevitably, further elements. The pit is cold; rabbits walk in and out of the pithead buildings. A raven flips and twists overhead. The bright-eyed optimism of new 'successor industry' units ('Biozyme' is a real but fictitious-sounding name attached to one of these on the outskirts of Blaenavon) betrays more than anything else the special development-zone status, the attempt to make things better once they have turned to the bad.

Here, at the exhausted end of the day, you cannot help feeling that this is a tragic landscape.

> **Distances in miles** *Rhymney to Tredegar 2.4; to Ebbw Vale 2.3; to Blaina 2.5; to Blaenavon 5.5.*
>
> **Map** OS *1:50,000, sheet 161, Abergavenny and the Black Mountains.*

2.

Where Two Landscapes Meet

Across Rutland

LEICESTERSHIRE

It would probably be wiser to do this long walk, about twenty miles from one edge of the old county of Rutland to the other, on a horse. Everything is tailored for horses here. The verges of the lanes are wide and gallopable, the horizons are long and inviting. The straight thorn hedges are everywhere trimmed into perfect, jumpable round-ness, like the piping on sofas.

But this is a walk; I do not like horses and, anyway, there is some pleasure to be had in being looked down at from the glossy back of a hunter. This is a long walk for a winter day and you have to go fast. Luckily, the landscape is right for it. You might see it (if this is not a little too flattering) as England's Wyoming, sodden with horse-culture, endless in its horizons. You can swing along from the border with Lincolnshire down the straight lane, past the fat sheep grazing in the pastures and the thorn trees distorted in the wind off the Lincolnshire Wolds to the village of Pickworth, a vestigial, half-abandoned place. It is back-end England here, with its empty, unadorned church and the atmosphere of rural depopulation still thick about it.

This is not pretty country but it has the attraction of unpreened and unpruned straightness, neither wild nor cosseted. As you walk down the long, straight track towards Leicestershire, the A1 and its lorries get gradually louder. Eventually, you reach the road with its grey lead-poisoned grasses and skip across into the woodbelts of the Exton estate, owned by Lord Gainsborough. This is the next element in the Rutland scene: the immensely grand. The maps of Rutland you will find on every pub wall in the old county show the elegant avenues, lakes and parkland of the Gainsborough estate. It is a little ragged now, but you can still get the picture. On the shores of a lake in the park is the charming 1785 Gothic summer house called Fort Henry, with picnic pinnacles and make-believe castellations. Not far from it are the earthworks in a field which are all that remain of a village that was once here, called Horn.

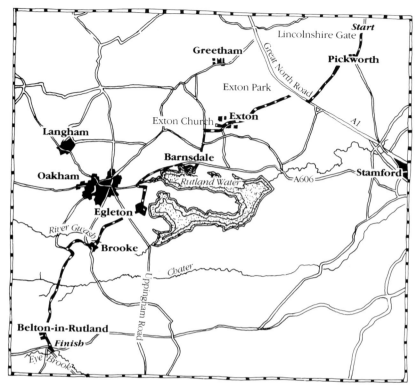

As you approach the village of Exton, you will find – again in a slightly broken state – an avenue of old and beautiful limes, their branches twisted and crinkled together in a knotted mass of Tina Turner hair, and their old boles extraordinarily sculpted in rounded overlapping ridges. Exton village itself is just beyond them, a pretty place, sitting demurely next to the wall of Exton Park, spacily arranged around a green filled with trees, half-thatched, half-roofed with the mouse-coloured Collyweston slates, with a pub, the Fox and Hounds Hotel, where as a man in the street said to me, 'they will sell you anything you want, but they will sell you it'.

Don't stay too long. The most wonderful sight in Rutland is just around the corner. Go through the village and up the lane through Lord Gainsborough's park to the church. Inside there is a series of monuments to members of the Harrington-Noel-Gainsborough family, from the early sixteenth century to the end of the eighteenth, which is unrivalled by any other small church in England. You could spend the whole day in this one church, moving from tomb to tomb;

The nineteenth-century New Hall in the park at Exton – a part of England where the seigneurial style survives undiminished.

the milky, still-medieval alabaster of John and Alice Harrington, he in his armour, she in the long, heavy pleats of a mantle, its hem picked up and played with by a pair of puppies; his head on a tasselled jousting helm, hers on a cushion, still bearing traces of its medieval paint. On to the pompous, polychrome marble monuments of a few decades later, with sausage-coloured columns and coffered niches, endless statuettes of dead babies kneeling by their parents and sonorous Latin descriptions; then, the arrival of the true spirit of seventeenth-century Italy, with the tomb of Anne, Lady Bruce, in white marble on a black plinth, her body carved realistically dead, one hand magically *under* the folds of the shroud, the fingers visible only as a slight rippling of the marble cloth.

You will now be behind time if you are to reach the other edge of Rutland before dark. The walk drops down to the edge of Rutland Water, the 3,500-acre reservoir, the biggest lake in England, created in the early 1970s by damming a small brook called the River Gwash. Its margins were carefully landscaped by Sylvia Crowe and there is no doubt that it is a beautiful place, its mushy, half-submerged edges covered with water birds, the Hambleton ridge rising apparently naturally out of it.

There is a path around the entire shore of the lake. Follow it until you leave the shores of Rutland Water and head for the small village of Egleton. (If you are fed up with walking and no lunch, you can detour up on to the Hambleton peninsula, where the most delicious food and wine in the English Midlands can be had in the extremely luxurious Hambleton Hall Hotel. But this is a radical option; there will be no continuing after lunch there. And I am not sure how they take to muddy boots either.)

A flock of geese rises over Rutland Water.

For the less sybaritic, Egleton village is a delight. Ziggurats of straw bales are piled in the mid-village yards. The air tingles with the sweet tang of silage. Topiary pheasants stick their bottoms out into Main Street. And the whole village is filled with beautiful vernacular architecture. Here you are on the border of the two Rutland landscapes: the hard, pale country of oolitic limestone, which you have crossed this morning; and the crumbly, softer, warmer country of the ironstone. The stones are brought together in the Egleton buildings: the body of the walls made of the rubbly orange ironstone, sometimes with veins of almost pure iron visibly twisted through a block; and the harder, whiter limestone used to pattern and strengthen them, as quoins and stringcourses, and as chimneys, mullions, doorposts and lintels.

The way to the far edge of Rutland, in the valley of the Eye Brook, lies across a series of three high ironstone ridges and the valleys that separate them. It is now that you long for a horse. Up on to Brooke Hill, with a beautiful view of the county town of Oakham in the Vale of Catmose, and then down across the River Gwash to the small village of Brooke, with a fascinating and unique church, part Norman, part Elizabethan, filled with original seventeenth-century joinery. But better than the church is the house half a mile outside it called Brooke Priory: I used to live a few miles from here and came on a weekly pilgrimage to lust after this beautiful place, with its half-crumbled Elizabethan brick walls, the ruined limestone gazebo in the garden, its long mossy Collyweston roof, its ironstone

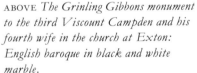

ABOVE *The Grinling Gibbons monument to the third Viscount Campden and his fourth wife in the church at Exton: English baroque in black and white marble.*

barn and stable yard, its position alone in the valley of the River Gwash, the big yews in its garden and the fantail pigeons fluttering between them.

But on; you will be hurrying now. Up to the next ridge, and down to the River Chater at Leigh Lodge. Then the last ridge before the valley of the Eye Brook and the old county border with Leicestershire. Rutland is never more beautiful than at this time of day and year, when every part of the landscape melts into a smoky, indeterminate brown, the colour of a border terrier's muzzle. Slither down in the encroaching dark to Belton-in-Rutland, a village that changes its name after Rutland became part of Leicestershire in 1974. It is almost entirely a commuter place. Walk down through the dark streets – it will surely be night by now – across the Leicester–Peterborough road, where the lit boxes of double-decker buses fill the rush-hour traffic, to the little stream beyond it. An ash tree hangs

The church at Egleton.

out over the water. Nothing marks the boundary here of what is now Rutland District and Harborough District, two sub-regions of Leicestershire.

Distances in miles *Lincolnshire Gate to Pickworth 0.8; to Great North Road 2.4; to Fort Henry 1.4; to Exton 1.6; to Exton Church 0.5; to Stamford Road 1.8; to Barnsdale 0.3; to Rutland Water 0.3; to lane to Egleton 2.0; to Egleton 1.0; to Uppingham Road 0.5; to Brooke 1.8; to Brooke Priory 0.6; to Leigh Lodge 2.3; to Belton-in-Rutland 2.3; to Eye Brook 0.7.*

Maps OS *1:50,000, sheets 130 (which covers Grantham and its surrounding area) and 141 (which includes Kettering and its surrounding area).*

3.

A Day in Soho

West End, London

The day begins in the Patisserie Valerie **1** (see map p. 26) on Old Compton Street. Chocolate roses dusted with icing sugar, boxed cakes on the shelves at the back, glazed strawberries under glass and, all around the room, red formica tables. At one of them Christine Keeler – I could have sworn it was her – was drinking a cappuccino. Or was it her daughter? She looked as beautiful as ever, her face a pale almond, her eyes oases of mascara. Perhaps it *was* her daughter. We did not speak, but my life will never be the same again.

Anyway, Valerie is *the* great place for media breakfasts, for the sweetest of rejecting goodbyes ('No doubt we'll be in touch – I feel there's a great deal of Kundera in what you've done ...') and the blatant swank ('I managed to get some studio space for Rob in Bucharest, but you know how he is, he just couldn't cope ...'). Style tips for Patisserie Valerie: try and read a copy of *Screen International*; practise the patient-resonance-of-the-actor voice, so that only five per cent of the sound comes out of your mouth – the rest must seem to come from somewhere under your chair; sideboards here should be long and Cretan-axe-shaped.

That was late breakfast. Next, round the corner into Greek Street, and up to the top end, on the very corner of Soho Square. Here is the House of St Barnabas **2**, the most interesting building in Soho, built in about 1746 and decorated a few years later by Richard Beckford, the brother of William Beckford of Fonthill. This house, which since 1862 has been a refuge for distressed women, is one of the best eighteenth-century interiors in London, a smooth succession of civilized and rational spaces, encrusted with rococo plaster, and with the most extraordinary addition at the back – a Cluniac-style, late nineteenth-century chapel, in perfect condition.

The charming Miss Edna Funnell (who remembers Zeppelins over the city and whose hero remains Ivor Novello) will show you round if you telephone her first (071-437 1894) to make a date. No style tips here except one: be nice to Miss Funnell.

Cappuccino at the Bar Italia, Frith Street: Milan translated intact to the middle of London.

On to a quick espresso in the Bar Italia **3** in Frith Street. Rocky Marciano looms over male Italians from a giant poster; Terence Trent D'Arby sings on Italian TV at the far end; the *patrone*, Nino, has one spectacular canine. Style: overtight black jeans, distressed leather, stubble, no women; you could try elements of the long-swept-back-lightly-oiled-hair look, with squarish hornrims, a dark grey corduroy suit, unironed shirt and pen in the outside jacket pocket (the Italo Calvino effect), but probably not all at once.

Then down to the south-east corner of Soho, past the rows of scarlet chickens and lacquered pigs of Chinatown, to Newport Court, where you will find Eoan of Merlins **4**, a soothsayer, up a little staircase at number 18. This street used to boast some small-time brothels and while Eoan was doing the tarot for me two men appeared at the door, realized things were not all they had hoped for and ran out again, groaning 'Oh my God, New Age....'

Eoan ignored them and continued with my future. the things she said were too bad to report. The Hanged Man was number two in the top row; I was in chaos and no one would ever love me again. Was she sure? No question about it.

It was time for relief. The French **5** in Dean Street used to be called the York Minster, but everyone knew it as the French and it was the most famous pub in Soho. It has now been renamed French House, redecorated with burgundy wallpaper, and has lost most of its previous allure, including its famous patron Gaston Berlemont. Style tip: think 'Anthony Burgess' and you won't go wrong. For me, things were not perfect. As I came in I saw at the bar a publisher I knew vaguely. A momentary eye-flick and he turned away to read the *Daily Telegraph*. Eoan had been right – life was on the slide.

More consolation was now required. Lunch at Quo Vadis **6** was only a short step up the street. This is a slightly difficult transition to make from the French. Everyone in Quo Vadis was in a suit and tie. Most people having lunch were, I think, 'consultants'. 'How are the MPs going?' a client asked at the next table. 'Soft', his fellow-suit replied.

Petto di Pollo Sophia Loren (she ate here once in the sixties) was very good, but the main purpose of lunch here was for the visit afterwards to the top floor – which is only allowed to patrons of the restaurant. A waiter will accompany you, three flights up from carpet to lino and then bare boards. The two top-floor rooms to the right of the staircase are the garret lodgings where Karl Marx, Jenny, the three children, their maid and nurse lived in poverty and squalor from 1850 to 1855. Two of his children died in these rooms while Marx was researching *Das Kapital*. If the revolution had ever come to Britain, this would have been a shrine; as it stands, filled with rubbish and spare furniture it is evocative enough.

Now, as the afternoon stretches ahead, there's a place a few yards down Dean Street to drop into for a while. Sunset Strip **7**, like Petto di Pollo Sophia Loren, is something of a survivor from another age – there has been a continuous performance here since 1960. Downstairs in the theatre thirty-odd blank-faced men, their lips sucked in over their lower teeth, sit in a couple of rows, a foot or two from a low stage. There is a divan on stage, and on the divan a woman. Not exactly a stripper, because no stripping actually happens. She is simply naked, begins naked and ends naked, without any progression.

There are lights in the floor of the stage so that no shadows obscure what the men are here to see. I stand at the back. The businessman in front of me – he wears a suit and smokes a little cigar – shifts himself up and to the right a little when the woman moves to lie on the floor, peering over the shoulder of the man in front of him so that he can see the whole thing. Among the others there is silence and no movement. She is noiseless too, except for the quiet sounds of the saliva on her lips and tongue as she mouths the words of the songs on the backing tape.

Next, down Meard Street **8**, the prettiest street in Soho. Its houses, once the most famous and disreputable brothels in London, have been smartened up and are now worth £500,000 each. Down Wardour Street to St Anne's churchyard **9**, simply to see the six-foot rise in ground level between the street and the churchyard; 10,000 corpses make the difference.

Back along Wardour Street, on the right-hand side of Walker

Raymond Revuebar at the bottom of Berwick Street and the inescapably male street-atmosphere of this part of Soho.

Court, you find a little doorway into Number 5, Dennis Cockell Exclusive Designs **10**. If he is not busy, Dennis will do you one on the spot, either a modern design or a full oriental backpiece, as you prefer. Nothing above the neck or below the wrist but anywhere else, just as you like it. You can bring your own ideas or he will execute one of the examples displayed on the wall, in many coloured inks. All is quite clean. Dennis Cockell is Soho's tattooist.

Moving swiftly on, Fish **11**, on D'Arblay Street, is a hairdresser which has kept, unchanged, the white-tiled setting of the fishmonger that used to occupy the premises. You might just like to look in at the window. There are more windows to investigate around the little courtyard called Portland Mews **12**, just along the street. This is dense media-ghetto, thick with post-production-location-editing-cum-casting suites. Glance through the windows and you see rows of men in their thirties talking on the telephone, ranks of them, all making the charm gestures they would be if they were meeting their victims in the flesh. But here, those persuasive twinkling eyes, those endearing movements of the arms and eyebrows, they all go to waste on the backs of men making exactly the same plays in front of them.

Around the corner in Poland Street **13** is one of the odder early evening sights of Soho. Just next to the Star and Garter (style tip:

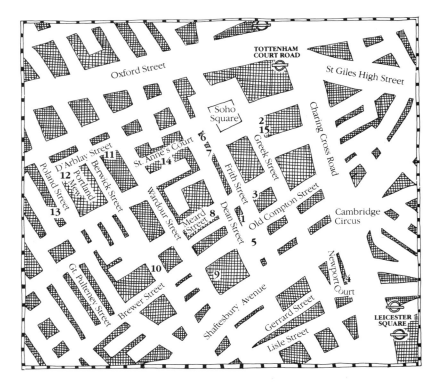

red, hot face, loosened tie; say 'it's been one hell of a week' and make Everest-summit-type grin) is Toppers, a famous topless bar. In the early evening the women who work at the bar arrive and enter through the front door.

If you want something a bit slicker, make your way over to Mitchell and O'Brien's **14** in St Anne's Court. This is a trendy American 1940s-type bar. Style tips: longish, straight sideboards, black cotton polo-necks under dark-grey suits, glasses that look like the front of a Peugeot; try to get the phrase 'in Prague . . .' into the sentence quite early on. The cocktails here are taken with a great deal of noise and it's the only bar in London in which there is not a single spotlight or downlighter to be seen. The result is cool gloom.

One last stop. Back into Soho Square, whose 1920s Tudor cottage is the spout for a ventilation shaft, over to the top of Greek Street and into the Gay Hussar **15**. This is the only real extravagance of the day – and the best part of it. Deep red squashy sofas, piled-up Magyar food, a thick and rather chummy atmosphere: it's as if all the exhibitionist voyeurism of the world outside doesn't exist.

4.

A Walk through Time

Marloes Sands

PEMBROKESHIRE

Perhaps the best walks don't go anywhere at all. They are not from somewhere to somewhere else; they simply poke around for a while in a single place, looking at what it has to offer, so that the walk itself ends up as a sort of day-long mooching, hanging around with a purpose.

Marloes Sands is a good place to mooch. It is a beach about a mile long almost on the western tip of Pembrokeshire. It can be a wild place in January, with huge south-westerly seas coming in unbroken from the Atlantic, dominated by that weird and inexplicable sensation on a stormy beach that the sea is higher than the beach itself, as though only some invisible barrier were preventing it from rolling in and swamping everything in its path. This is the Atlantic margin on the grand scale; set sail from these sands and your next arrival would be Brazil.

But Marloes Sands is not simply a beach. For geologists it is one of the classic locations. Here, very clearly, is one of the places in the British Isles where the history of the rocks that make up the landscape is most dramatically on show. Yet the fields that lead down to the beach from the village of Marloes are flat and ordinary: there is no hint whatsoever of the complex rock structures that lie beneath them. It is all sheep and hedges and schoolmasters leaning out of the youth hostel windows.

But arrive at the coast and it all changes. The beach is not a beach but a brutal chaos of broken stones; only the slivers of grey-yellow sand between the rocks look easy and hospitable. The spray from the breaking Atlantic merges with the mist. The island of Skokholm is hazed by it in the mid-distance; nearer at hand the little island of Gateholm stands out more sharply at the western end of the beach. Only slowly from this heap of stony rubbish does a sense of structure begin to emerge.

The whole place, in two periods of mountain-building about 400 million and 250 million years ago, has been seriously crumpled. The

ABOVE *Between high and low tide the rocks emerge encrusted in barnacles and mussels.*

PREVIOUS PAGE *Stacked like slates in a builder's yard, the rocks at Marloes Sands are the roots of mountains long since eroded away.* Inset: *Even on the most wintry of days the beach is rarely empty of someone looking for something the sea has thrown up.*

rock layers, which began as a succession of sea-floors, are set near-vertical in the cliffs and outcrops on the beach, like stacks of slates in a builder's yard. They are the roots of a great upward fold of rock that stretched northwards from here to St Bride's Bay.

A later sea planed off the crest of this rock-wave to leave the

inland parts of the peninsula almost as flat as Bedfordshire. Only at the coast does the history of cataclysm appear. These are mountain-roots, on show because the sea is again eating away at Pembrokeshire.

The crumpling on both occasions, the result of warring collisions between now long-forgotten continental masses, lasted for an immensely long time – perhaps one hundred million years each. It was a slow hard squeeze. Wherever you look there are signs of the rock suffering this long-drawn-out stress – networks of hairline fractures gridding the whole surface of rock bodies; shear-faults where the elasticity of the material reached breaking point and the rock tore apart; the curve of rock cracking like a piece of drying clay, opening up a rough little crevice where previously it had been a rounded unbroken surface; tiny penetrative veins of quartz squeezing themselves in between the finest laminations of the mother rock. Some of the veins are visibly rusty; others are stained a light, coppery green. These ever-present veins are all that remain of hot, mineral-bearing liquids that forced themselves into the older stone under the intense heat and pressure of the earth movements beneath them.

But there is far more to Marloes Sands than the evidence of past mountain-chains. The original sequence of rocks that was laid down one on top of another here between 400 and 500 million years ago, before any mountain-building episodes interfered with them, is still plainly there, if turned through ninety degrees.

Grasp one element in the Marloes rockscape and all becomes clear: what was once vertical is now horizontal; what was once horizontal is now vertical. A series of layers on the sea floor is now a sequence of rock types arranged side by side in the cliffs, lined up along the back of the beach like a collection of geological volumes in a library. The sequence as it was laid down was about 3,000 feet thick, and is now, as you walk beside it along the sands, about 1,000 yards from end to end.

In amazingly precise detail you can find yourself walking through – or at least beside – the evolving landscape of south Wales as it was when the first bony fishes were swimming in the sea and the earliest plants were beginning to colonize the land. A walk along Marloes Sands is a walk through a whole landscape and seascape seen through the medium of time.

The place where you should begin is a broad and grassy scoop in the cliff-line, known as Mathew's Slade, 300 or 400 yards east of the point where the path from Marloes village reaches the beach. From Mathew's Slade, time moves eastward along the cliff.

First **1** (see map opposite) are some yellow-grey sandstones, the floor of a quite shallow sea, the oldest environment represented here, perhaps 500 million years old and curiously like the sands of the modern beach. These were the floors of an inshore sea near a big block of mainland somewhere to the south-east.

A hundred yards along the cliff these sandstones are cut through by two lava flows in the form of reddish-black basalts **2** in a little gully. The lava flow is enormously thick, at least sixty feet, and geologists think that it probably came from an island volcano somewhere to the north-west of here and only a mile or two away.

After the lava flows comes a period **3** – a stretch of cliff about 100 yards long – of a very murky and muddy sea, whose bed was made of grey-green sludge and fine sands, in which occasionally, where a section of rock has flaked away, one can make out the ripples on the face of an ancient sea floor.

Like the sandstones before them these mudstones are interrupted, about 75 yards after the basalt lava flows, by bands **4** of a rock which geologists call tuff – the compressed residue of the pebbly ash which was pumped out of the island volcano and fell into the sea. It was a huge eruptive spasm: the tuff layer is nearly twenty feet thick.

Beyond the trio of monumental sandstone bands known as Three Chimneys **5** a broad pattern emerges: the sea starts to dry out. Layers of the sands now held rigid in stone are seen to be 'cross-bedded' – they were near enough to the surface of the sea not to be laid down in regular horizontal sheets but in patterns whose grain runs first one way and then the other.

In the roof of a small cave **6** beds rich in fossils of an inshore coral reef are revealed. Beyond those coral-thick bands a succession of brown, grey-green and yellow mudstones and siltstones **7** are, for the amateur, very difficult to understand, but certain aspects of them hint to geologists that what you are seeing here, as you clamber over the wreckage of cliff falls and the slithery skin of oarweed and bladderwrack, is the history of a river encroaching on a sea.

Here are deposits in shallow water; the muds of a delta combined with the sands and salt-mud of the zone between the tides; and eventually the muddy wetlands of a river valley as the land extends out into part of the planet's surface, which had been sea for tens of millions of years. We might perhaps be looking at something like the growth of the Mississippi delta into the Gulf of Mexico.

The transition from marine deposits, which are grey here, to the muds laid down by river floods on land is marked **8** by a large arrow carved in the cliff-face by the Geological Survey. Beyond the arrow are the huge ruddy cliffs of one of the most famous rocks of all, the Old Red Sandstone. The Red Sandstone cliffs at Hooper's Point close off the south-eastern end of Marloes Sands.

One could repeat this exercise time and time again on the Pembrokeshire coast, but if this walk is about anything, it is about the great pleasure to be had from going very, very slowly indeed. If you have got the timing of the tides right, the best place from which to survey the sands is up on the top of Gateholm, at the other end of the bay, which you can reach at low tide. (Do not get cut off!)

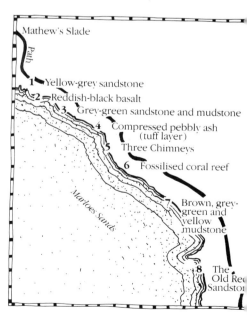

Map OS *1:25,000 sheet* SM *70, Skomer Island.*

Guidebooks Geological Excursions in Dyfed, Southwest Wales, *ed. M G Bassett, National Museum of Wales, 1982 (a technical but expert field guide to many geologically interesting places in south Wales, including Marloes Sands).* British Regional Geology, South Wales, HMSO *1970, gives the broader picture.*

5.

Temples and Towpaths

The Gloucester–Sharpness Canal

GLOUCESTERSHIRE

If you are lucky, this short walk through the depths of the Vale of Berkeley in the west of Gloucestershire will begin very well.

Stand on the swing-bridge over the Gloucester and Sharpness Canal outside the village of Frampton-on-Severn. Next to you on the canal bank is a little Doric temple – the bridge-keeper's house, built in 1827 at the same time as the canal, with a pair of columns for its portico and a wide pediment balanced over them. This waterway, with a width of nearly ninety feet and a draught of eighteen feet, was, at the time it was built, the largest ship canal in the world, able to take vessels of more than 600 tons from the Bristol Channel to the docks at Gloucester, avoiding the bends and shifting sandbanks of the River Severn and giving access to the network of canals in the industrial Midlands. This is a fine marriage of the best and purest of neo-classical architecture and the highest of early industrial technology. Thomas Telford, if not very closely involved, was the overseeing engineer. You will enjoy this place for that atmosphere alone.

But then – and this is where the luck comes in – you will hear, not knowing quite what it is at first, the most sublime of sounds, the drifting fullness of Fauré or Bach, coming out of the basement of the Doric temple to float over the umbrella-hooded fishermen, as they sit watching their motionless floats. The bridge-keeper plays the organ.

You can start off down the canal bank, but that would be to miss the village of Frampton. So make an immediate detour away from the canal, past the works of the Frampton Village Cider Company (the most sweet-smelling industrial site in England) and down the road to the opening of the village green, which, with its wide lawn of nibbled turf stretching out of sight southwards, comes as a great and generous surprise. Along its eastern side there is a many-windowed castellated Gothic orangery (1745) with a tower and a cupola, many ivy-soaked trees and a long park wall. All this belongs

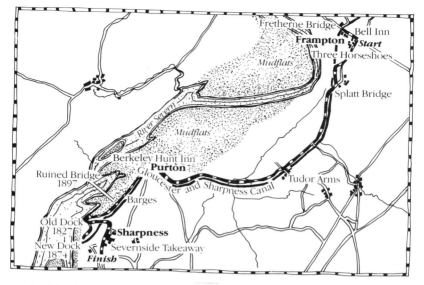

to the big house, Frampton Court. You can see the house beyond its wall, raised on a high basement and flanked by twin chimneys-cum-belltowers.

This is the smart side of Frampton. Lining the opposite edge of the long green, like tenants in front of the local grandee, are the other houses of the village. There are many excellent buildings here, too: the tall Georgian post office, a town house dumped in a field; the manor and its beautiful cross-timbered barns, with orchards glimpsed at the back; the highly eccentric recent barn conversion at the bottom end of the green; and a little brick house with a slightly wobbly and provincial version of a Venetian window set in the middle of its façade. This combination of very pretty buildings with the entrancing openness of its plan has made the village a magnet for incomers. There is a smartish restaurant called Savery's here now (as well as The Bell and the Three Horseshoes).

A lich-gate halfway down the village opens on to an avenue of old and ragged chestnuts leading across a damp field to the church (locked) and then on to the canal bank at Splatt Bridge. The towpath stretches straight ahead. Over to the west, the blue hills of the Forest of Dean; to the east the darker woods of the Cotswold edge. This is a reservoir of placidity, an evacuated, aqueous motorway where for miles there is nothing but the pollarded willows and the sheep fattening on the salty turf, the witter of duck and, at this time of year, the Bewick's swans nibbling in the winter meadows. Not a

Kathleen Musslewhite serves a customer in the Berkeley Hunt Inn at Purton.

yard of ploughed land is to be seen; it is far too wet for that. At each bridge there is another Doric pavilion, looking as if it should be on an antiquarian's desk, as neat as an inkstand.

Walk on down the canal for another couple of miles, past the waterworks that draw water out of the canal and send it underground to Bristol, to the tiny village of Purton. The canal splits the village down the middle. There is a pub here, the Berkeley Hunt Inn, its garden gate on the canal side, and its atmosphere – rare enough now – not interfered with. It is, as many pubs used to be, scarcely distinguishable from a farmhouse. There is no bar in the room where you sit down; the place to buy a drink or a sandwich is a small counter at the end of the passageway leading from the front door. No machines, no music, no fake rusticity here.

Just beyond Purton, in a smooth and fluid coming-together, the canal slides up to meet the edge of the Severn and runs alongside it. Between the two waters there is nothing but a fragile bank, washed by fast and heavy tides – the second strongest in the world.

To counter the erosion, the canal company shored up the embankment in the most remarkable of ways. The hulks of many barges – the older ones wooden, the newer steel and concrete – have been driven ashore here on a high tide. There must be fifty of them now; a school of whales forced out of the sea to a communal grave. Their

Earth-filled barges reinforce the banks of the canal as it edges along the Severn Estuary approaching Sharpness.

holds have been filled with earth, and around some of them it has been piled up to the gunwales so that these rotten vessels seem sunk in a grass sea. On the transom of one you can still make out the words, divided by the rudder, HARRIET: BRISTOL, cut into the timber one hundred years ago or more.

You are now on the last leg of this walk to Sharpness, the port at the canal's mouth into the Severn. As the tide drops, the smooth lobes of sandbanks and the looping channels between them emerge to pattern the width of the river to your right.

You pass by the epic ruins of the Severn Railway Bridge, first opened in 1897, and intended to bring coal from the Forest of Dean coalfield for export and refuelling of ships in Sharpness. Its twenty-two spans survived until November 1959, when two oil tankers, making for the difficult entrance to Sharpness in a heavy flood tide, were carried past and slammed into the central piers, demolishing two spans. Both tankers exploded, covering the river with burning oil and killing both crews. The bridge was finally demolished in 1967 and the girders sold to Chile, where they are still in use as a road viaduct. All you can see now is the stump of a pier or two in midstream at low tide and, by the canal, the substructure of the swing-bridge which used to open to allow the tall-masted ships to

The curving arms of the breakwaters beyond the lockgates at Sharpness.

pass through to Gloucester.

After the bridge, you are almost into Sharpness. The path swings round with the canal to the Old Dock. It is disused, a beautiful place where the Old Dock House, a neo-classical building and the father of all the bridge houses along the canal, is being allowed to rot away.

By the 1860s, the old dock had become too small for the size of ship and the volume of traffic using the canal. It was decided to build a new one, opened in 1874, and it is on that new dock that this walk ends. It is the last surprise of all – here in rural Gloucestershire, the farms coming close up to it, a working industrial port, gritty and dirtied, where concrete bulk-carriers registered in Nassau lie alongside the dusty warehouses; where giant windowless silos, designed in Kansas City, stand by the quays; where mounds of rusted turnings from Midlands machine shops lie waiting for export; where thousands of bags of Norwegian fishmeal are stacked; where corrugated iron has been crushed into hundreds of cube-shaped blocks, destined for a buyer somewhere.

Sharpness is not in decline: a plasterboard factory is under construction and an area of red-brick industrial housing is on the point of demolition to make way for further industrial sites. A dry dock is fully functioning as a repair yard. The village of Sharpness – that rare thing in southern England, an industrial village – is up on the hill to the east. That is where you should end, as the sun drops into Wales, eating fish and delicious chips in the newly-opened, locally-owned Severnside Takeaway.

Distances in miles *Fretherne Bridge to Bell Inn, Frampton 0.4; to Frampton Church 0.9; to Tudor Arms, Shepherds Patch 2.1; to Berkeley Hunt Inn, Purton 2.5; to ruined railway bridge 1.2; to Sharpness harbour mouth 1.5; to Severnside Takeaway, Sharpness 1.5.*

Map *OS 1:50,000, sheet 162, Gloucester and Forest of Dean.*

6.

Are We Having Fun Yet?

A Family Disaster in Dartmoor

DEVON

Looking back on it now, I think this scheme might have been a little ambitious. The other people in the hotel were full of mature, if quite discreet, premonition. 'I won't say it's not a disappointing day,' the narrow Scotswoman said at breakfast, as Devon drivelled down outside the window. 'But then there is a charm to Dartmoor when it's raining quite as heavily as it has been for the past few weeks. The moor's in its element when it is soaking wet, is it not?' I chose not to react. From the train on the way down the previous afternoon, we had seen nothing but sodden fields for a hundred miles. The Somerset wetlands had for once lived up to their name; the Exe valley had been a lake. Despite these warnings, we had a plan and we were, for the moment anyway, going to stick to it: a winter walk *and night out* on Dartmoor with two small children. With eiderdowns up over the bedheads and sleeping bags instead of sheets and blankets, the entire family had been practising for weeks.

This was the party: Olivia my wife, twenty-eight, Thomas, very nearly five, William, two and a half, and me, thirty-one. We had chosen the place very carefully, knowing that the main competition here was neither the South Downs nor the Peak district, but the Thundercats video. I know the film well. Its grip on my sons' imagination depends on two things: continuous and rather attractive violence; and nothing lasting longer than fifteen seconds. How could a walk, that most unviolent and continuous of things, how could it hope to compete with this? How near, in fact, could the English landscape ever get to Thundercats-Ho – The Movie?

I had to be realistic. Any attempt to introduce less-than-five-year-olds to the nuanced charms of the natural world would not be a success. We have to challenge the electronic media on their own terms. The only possible place, I decided, thinking of eighteenth-century romanticists shuddering at the horrors of Gothic nature, was the deep valley of a fast-running stream, with boulders and frothing water in its bed and a path along the banks from which one

Adam, William (seated), Olivia and Thomas contemplate the flood.

William eats his third Mars Bar of the morning.

could view the rude shocks of nature in complete safety. The warmest version of this in England was likely to be in south Dartmoor. I scoured the map. The valley of the River Avon above Shipley Bridge seemed to have everything that was needed – a deep curving valley, a drop for the stream of 170 feet in less than a mile, high moorland on either side, and a good wide track along the banks, the nearest the outside world could ever come to that Marmite-stained sofa in front of the TV.

It started like a dream. The monsoon was coming down. Dartmoor was leaking like a wrestler in a sauna; every pore a fountain, every surface a sheen of water. Our equipment was perfect, all four of us dry inside a glistening plastic skin. My large new rucksack, described by the salesman as 'this highly adaptive load suspension system', was living up to its name, the entire sleeping arrangements for my family hanging unnoticed on my back. Thomas was carrying the chocolate, William his lavatory equipment, Olivia the stoves and food. Then the first problem: William did not understand that the idea was to walk somewhere in a straight line. In fact, everything he could ever have wanted was to be found in a large puddle on the edge of the car park. This, anyway, we had predicted: it would not be wise to attempt any real progress on our walk. As far as the children were concerned, staying in the same place for a very long time would be just as good. So for three-quarters of an hour, that is exactly what we did. William's rolled-up waterproof trousers slumped around his ankles. His woollen hat did very well for a few minutes as a raft on which leaves could be piled until it sank in the puddle. His face and then his hands turned pink. Olivia and I stood around as wallflowers while William partied. It occurred to me that there might be something not entirely heroic about hanging about in a tourist car park on the edge of Dartmoor dressed for the south face of Annapurna. On cue, an old lady with a beige umbrella, pushing her grandson in a buggy in front of her, eased past me in my Berghaus Mountain cagoule and under my Swedish high-tech load suspension system. 'Going for a walk?' she asked disingenuously. It was not a good moment. William was still exploring the deltaic system at the bottom end of the car park. Something had to give. It was Tom that broke: 'For Christ's sake, when the hell are we going to go camping?' he said, rather impressively. 'Now,' I said, and we set off.

The valley of the Avon was wet and beautiful. The river was in spate, brown and roaring over the rocks in its bed. It was everything any Thundercat fan could ever have wanted, innocuous and terrifying at the same time. 'Water,' William said, more awed by this than by anything since Father Christmas in Debenhams last year. On the far side, a deep Victorian planting of rhododendrons; on this side, a brown and rounded moor. Tom and I walked up the gentle path together, with the river to one side and, on the other, a small tributary stream with a gravelly bed, only a foot or so wide, a perfect racecourse for stick boats. A rather scraggly gorse bush here provides big sticks, old bracken small ones. The stick-racing contributed about six minutes supply to Tom's frighteningly heavy entertainment habit. Then it was ever onward and upward again.

For a few minutes, William and Olivia caught us up. There is a small rock face here, where the moor comes down near the river-bank. Tom climbed it;

Adam collects water from the river for a space-food lunch.

Olivia fainted. William walked about on a big flat slab of granite half in the stream, so that the falling water slivered over his boots. He was not keen on holding hands, screaming instead the worst insult he could think of at the moment: 'YOU ARE.' I took it on the chin and he then allowed me to walk about with him here for a moment or two, chasing rhododendron leaf boats, feeling – as the sun came out! – that this entire pantomime was finally worth it.

Thomas, returned from the rock face, was now desperate to pitch camp. Together we deserted the others and set out to find a good spot. Dartmoor is overgrazed. Acres of it are chewed up with pony hooves and covered in large brown piles of dung. Tom sank into despair. I tried to banish any thoughts of bed and breakfast from my mind and to consider camping on this brown morass. One small patch in the mouth of a small quarry under Woolholes would have been ideal except for two enormous piles of what Tom rather sweetly called horse-done. We tried kicking them away. They disintegrated on contact into little brown specks covering what had been an otherwise perfectly green campsite. It was now a health hazard.

We broke out the Kendal Mint Cake and felt gloomy. More grannies walked past. Thomas felt cold. At last I found a place for the tent, right next to, but a few feet above, the river, dung-free, perfect. The high-tech lightweight Ultimate Equipment Horizon B (our tent) was up and out in a matter of minutes. Olivia hallooed us from a distant hill where she had pursued William pursuing sheep. 'Is this camping fun?' Thomas asked in his new rhetorical style. 'YES IT IS.'

Next the excellent Swedish Trangia lightweight meths-stove-cum-integration-pot-system for the dehydrated space-food lunch. Olivia and William arrived, a little worse for wear, but nothing that Kendal Mint Cake couldn't cure. Tom scooped up water from the river and then threw a cup in to see if I could get it back again. By mistake we cooked up Hungarian Goulash with Paprika *and* Cornish Rice Pudding with Raisins at the same time in the same pot. It tasted very nice, as this sort of food always does taste in the middle of nowhere. I secretly think the only things they vary are the labels.

Here was contentment: every bush and rock for yards around covered in drying clothes; a pale sun; the wet brown moors around us; re-hydrated lunch; insulation mats and sleeping bags making the tent warm and welcoming; no fighting or tent destruction (although this is a danger permanently on the brink of erupting); washing up after lunch in the stream; a little whisky. What could be better?

But then we made a mistake. The three of them looked soporific, nuzzled inside the tent and their sleeping bags. I decided to leave them – the inevitable fatherly escape which every family will know too well – and to go for a walk. It was wonderful, high up on the snowy tops of the moors, with a view out southwards to the sunlit Channel and the green folds of Devon dropping towards it. I walked for about four miles over the moor, around the head of the Avon Reservoir, fording the river above it (too cold and too deep – halfway up the thighs) and then back down by the Avon Dam to the campsite. Snow was just flecking around the tent as I reached it. I peered inside. It looked like the sort of charity advertisement published early in December: 'Olivia, Thomas and William are still looking forward to Christmas this year,' the caption would have said, 'even without a proper roof over their heads.' There had been fighting. A disintegrated nappy lay under the flysheet. Kendal Mint Cake papers littered the inside. Feeling like Bonnington at Camp Five, I suggested a withdrawal. The snow, rather beautifully in the dusk, was floating down like scraps of paper around us. Everyone agreed: back to the car park. We packed and tidied up, scuffed the flattened grass upright and then skipped off down the track. Thomas confessed, whisperingly, that it might have been rather frightening anyway, mightn't it, sleeping out there, because you never know, even with X-ray vision, what there might be, do you? And as I walked back down beside the Avon, with the load suspension system resettled on my shoulders, the snow thickening on the path, and a filled nappybag in either hand, I felt that it had been a very good day indeed.

Map OS *1:25,000 Outdoor Leisure 28 (Dartmoor)*.

Equipment *If you are going to attempt this sort of expedition, you have to carry with you a very complete child protection kit. Lack of the right equipment will mean disaster. A large tent, a large modern rucksack and good sleeping bags are expensive, but it is unthinkable without them as it is without such items as stoves, fuel, waterproof matches, lightweight pots and pans, mugs, spoons, torches, adequate food (freeze-dried) and sweets, complete waterproof clothing, changes of clothes, towels, nappies etc.*

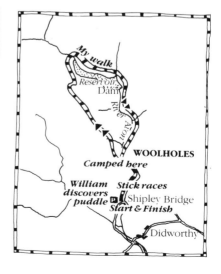

7.

The River Calder from
Mouth to Source

Sellafield to Ennerdale Water

CUMBRIA

This walk along the River Calder, from mouth to source, begins on the edge of the Irish Sea and ends at the point where the river that has accompanied you all day shrinks to a trickle and then sidles into nothing, high in the western fells of the Lake District.

You start on the coast at Seascale, with the most radioactive sea in the world on your left and the golf links on your right. Ahead is a dazzling sorcerer's kitchen, the combined towers of Calder Hall nuclear power station and the Sellafield nuclear fuel reprocessing plant, all gathered around the cooling waters of the Calder.

It is glamorous before the dawn. The steam from the cooling towers builds into monumental clouds, lit yellow from the sodium lights below them. The cranes on the vast new site where thousands of men are engaged in making Sellafield one of the biggest plants of its kind in the world, are speckled with red and green lights. It is a vision on a universal scale planted in west Cumbria: something quite indifferent to the local world around it. Sellafield would look the same if it were in Windhoek, Namibia, or on the surface of Mars. It is that mixture of self-sufficiency and unintelligibility which gives so much impetus to the fear of nuclear power.

Its appearance – the fences, the policemen, the lights, the busyness (14,000 people are employed here), the small blue containers in which the spent fuel arrives by rail, the mysterious processes, part revealed in the outline of tubes and cylinders and the unprettified structures – all this, as the Isle of Man comes up out of the dark to the west of you, and the curlews can be heard beyond the dunes, makes you feel like a spy.

The river slides out between the atomic architecture and spills over the shingle to the sea. The river water is not noticeably warm. Pick up eleven small pebbles here and put them in your rucksack.

The map shows pale little lanes snaking up by the river towards Calder Bridge, but these are no longer rights of way and you have to edge around the forbidden zone for about three miles until you

The drama of modern technology at the Sellafield nuclear processing plant.

can get back to the river. The policemen on the gates are quite firm about this. On the way you cross over the half-sunken pipelines, through which the contaminated water discovered by Greenpeace once flowed, and then pass under the powerlines going north to the national grid – together the twin products of the place.

These roads are not particularly pleasant – they are small lanes turned into dual carriageways for the nuclear traffic – but just short of Calder Bridge, quite unexpectedly, beyond a low wall made of half-rounded river cobbles, you come on the Calder again, where the sound of water over rock and the sunshine on its broken surface is a sudden relief.

Calder Bridge is almost nothing: a rather ugly church in red sandstone, the Stanley Arms, and the post office, where you can get a Mars bar or two. Here you can join the river, with its salmon and sea-trout in the deep holding pools (or so they tell me), as it makes a wide sweep up its valley, through diminishing layers of wealth and comfort. First there is the parkland of Calder Abbey, slightly ragged, the trees with decrepit limbs, the grazing muddied by the cattle and the house itself, the eighteenth century brick block attached to the mossy ruins of the medieval abbey, with a cold and neglected air.

Beyond that, the way climbs along the eastern side of the valley. (There is an alternative up the western side but it will mean fording

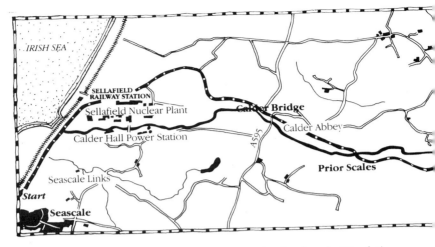

RIGHT *The sheep-nibbled ruins of Calder Abbey, abandoned at the Dissolution, used as a quarry for farm-buildings ever since.*

the river a little higher up beyond Thornholme.) You pass a string of farms. Don't miss the beautiful red sandstone barn at Prior Scales, with its built-in dovecote and unshiftable solidity. The river is far below, still broad but now gravelly, here and there braided into separate streams and stony, leaf-shaped islands.

Beyond Thornholme comes the great change in the river. Worm Gill goes off to the east and leaves the Calder only half its previous size. It becomes an upland river, small enough to be knowable, breaking in small waterfalls through dykes of harder rock, crossed in one of these narrow places with a single, rather rickety medieval stone arch called Monk's Bridge, and then meandering for miles through the flat bottom of its valley. Constantly, small streams leach away from the river, up into the peaty dampness of Kinniside Common and Latterbarrow Moss. The mist comes down and the river is jumpable, the width of a table. Now you can straddle it as it sleeks between the moor-grasses, rounded like the back of an otter. The Herdwick sheep, the gloomiest of all English breeds, have never seen anyone up here. The stream – it is nothing more now – goes underground for a yard or two and everything is liquid and mossy. The definition begins to go.

And then you have arrived. A black patch of raw peat decorated here and there with clumps of primitive moss like vegetable brains: this is the source of the Calder, one of the hags in a messy bit of northern England called Black Pots. Here you can deposit your

46

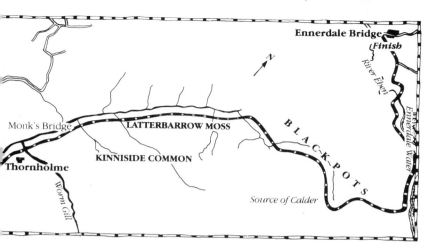

pebbles from the river's mouth, one for every mile you have come.

To get back to Seascale, take a taxi from Ennerdale Bridge where there's a pub, a post office, a telephone and another river, the Ehen, whose mouth is within 200 yards of the Calder's.

Distances in miles *Seascale Links to mouth of Calder 1; to Sellafield station 0.8; to Calder Bridge 2.8; to Calder Abbey 0.7; to Prior Scales 0.9; to Thornholme 1; to source of Calder 5.4; to Ennerdale Water 1.1; to Ennerdale Bridge 3.2.*

Map *OS 1:50,000, sheet 89, West Cumbria.*

8.

Desert Days

Canyonlands National Park

UTAH

It looks like Mars, but Mars dressed in the colours of America: steak-red rock, a spangling of white clouds, and over-arching it all the utter blue of the Utah sky. The silence is extreme and the middle of the day sounds like midnight. All you hear are the movements of your own body, the scuffing of your boots in the dust, your own heart and breath, the sticking of the butt of a cigarette to your drying lips. This is the American wilderness, as empty now as it has ever been. Two hundred thousand people a year visit the Canyonlands National Park in south-eastern Utah but the park rangers reckon that only one per cent of them ever get out of their Air Stream trailers or their fat-wheeled high-riding trucks, except to go to the loo or peer out from an overlook. To walk in the fretted and broken 500 square miles of the park, you must be prepared to be alone.

It is a mountain landscape in the negative. Here you must descend to get away. The roads are laid across the top of a high plateau, a fat cake of ancient rocks, which extends over the state lines into Arizona, New Mexico and Colorado. It would be quite possible to drive from Salt Lake to Phoenix and never know what extraordinary things lay beneath and beside you. What is there is the work of the two great rivers of the south-west, the Green and the Colorado, fed by the snows in the Wind River Mountains of Wyoming and the high Rockies. Here, heading for the Gulf of California, they cross dry country, where less than ten inches of rain falls every year. It is that simple meeting – erosive rivers in a semi-desert – which has created the canyons. In a rainier country, with many tributary streams and rivulets, and with the softening of vegetation to bind the rock and soil, the surrounding land would have come down to meet the rivers in smoothed and easy transitions. There are none here; this is a place of cliffs and trenches, of abruptness and definition which is more like a city than a piece of the natural earth, of rivers and sudden thunderstorm rain that have worked on the landscape like an acid.

But this is not Peru. The park – and even the idea that this hostile,

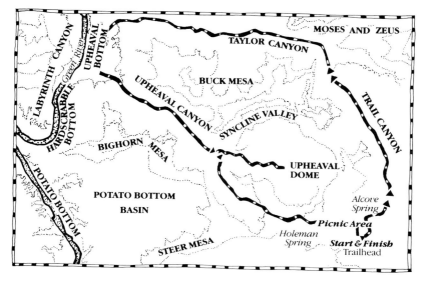

uncompromised place could be called a park is odd – is as organized in its way as an airport terminal. There is an element of nannying and mollycoddling in the manner with which the National Park Service treats its visitors. The roads they have provided are large sweeping highways, not rough tracks. The shampooed and laundered ranger in the Visitor Center will grant you a Backcountry Use Permit (which you must tie to your rucksack), tell you what to do with 'human waste' (bury it deep), loo paper (pack it out), how much water to carry (a gallon a person a day), where not to go, when you can leave, when you must be back, where to camp (out of sight), what not to touch, what souvenirs not to collect – before you are admitted to what she cheerfully describes as 'the wilderness'. It comes near enough to castrating the experience before it has begun.

You can safely forget all that. When the walk does begin, the canyons reveal themselves as raw. This is not the place for laundry. It is only twelve miles from the head of the Alcove Spring Trail in the north-western corner of the park to the banks of the Green River but it takes the best part of a day to get there. The heat, even in the springtime, is thickening, soporific. The drop into the canyon, from about 5,500 to about 4,000 feet, is scrabbly and difficult. You soon reach the spring after which the trail is named. It doesn't actually flow but leaks a few drips like a tap with the washer gone. All the same, the dribbling spring – and this is a mark of the physical instability of this place – has eroded an oval half-dome in the cliff

above it a hundred yards across, fifty deep and fifty high. This huge and shadowed hole in the cliff is the 'alcove' after which the spring is named. In a landscape where everything is enormous, the only recourse is to understatement. No wonder Marlboro men are famous for saying nothing; there's far too much to say.

Fraying ropy-barked junipers and the occasional *piñon* pine stand around the line of the wash that meanders in the bed of the canyon. The rock walls beyond them are the colour of raw meat gone dry. It is a brutal place, where the snub-noses of the buttresses that line the walls of Trail Canyon look like the rusted prows of an abandoned fleet. The new leaves of the cottonwoods down on the wash are the only signs of freshness in a place that seems to have grown old simply

The Green River curls within the dry and fretted landscape of the Canyonlands.

through drought. It would be easy to imagine that no one had ever been here. Gashes cut into the canyon walls, of the size and drama of the most famous beauty spots in Europe, have no name.

But look at the map more carefully and you will begin to read some of the history of the pioneer Americans who came here. It was a virtually unentered country before 1869 when Major John Wesley Powell made the first successful and terrifying journey down the Green River and then, after its junction with the Colorado, through the Grand Canyon. His names for the reaches of the river here – Labyrinth Canyon, Stillwater Canyon – remain on the map today, the simple transcription of the feelings and experiences which he and his party had in the place. Occasionally they named more grandly: Cleopatra's Chair is what they called a high and isolated butte far to the west of the river. It can indeed look like a giant rock-throne.

A second layer of names, perhaps from a decade or two afterwards, overlies that first moment in the written history of the canyonlands. A huge tract of half-desert is called simply Ernie's Country. Who else could have wanted it? Bobby's Hole, Pappy's Pasture, Sweet Alice Canyon, Pete's Mesa – these are the names of places where no one is now to be found. In this extraordinarily accelerated version of history, one can read the names of the great-grandparents, in all probability, of people now alive, but who are as forgotten, as absent from the place they called their own, as the Saxon leaders after whom villages in England are named. This could never have been a place to be owned. To have named something so inhospitably arid as if it could be possessed could only ever have been a gesture of hope. On the map one can also read names which more exactly describe how things must have been: Hardscrabble Bottom, Horsethief Canyon, Deadhorse Canyon, Deadman Canyon, Hell Roaring Canyon.

After a few hours, Trail Canyon opens out into Taylor Canyon. Two rock pinnacles called Moses and Zeus, a pair of red and shattered tombstones many hundreds of feet high, mark the place. The canyons merge like urban freeways, the cliffed masses standing around them in city blocks. I ate my lunch and listened to the unaccustomed noise of one's own eating. The cauliflower clouds of a thunderstorm built to the south-west, their rims lit, their bellies black. In the silence a piece of rock, perhaps the size of a house, fell from the cliff a mile away on the far side of Taylor Canyon in a series of thudding bangs like someone hitting a table with a mallet.

I lay and slept for a while on a rock which bore the ripples of the sea that had laid it down. As I kicked my heels against it, the rock disintegrated again after 150 million years or so into the sand particles of which it was made. I woke to see a man in a four-wheel drive Subaru looking at me. He had a beer in his hand. We talked about desert walking. 'I'd like you to see this,' he said. I thought he was going to show me another geological curiosity. He was. He lifted up his shirt and revealed his stomach. 'I like to think of it as a mesa,' he said and held it like a butcher with a piece of tripe. 'I suppose I'd better look for a camp,' he said. 'Yes,' I said brutally. 'I suppose you'd better.' I was not game for a mesa-dominated evening. 'You look as if you've been out here for weeks,' he said and drove away towards Bighorn Point.

The solitary sleep in the desert – perhaps that is the best thing of all. I had no tent and lay down in my sleeping bag on the scratchy gravel of the earth. This place, Upheaval Bottom, is a level bench next to the river, ringed with cliffs and the slopes below them of broken rock. It was a clear evening and, as the colour went from the sky above and the rocks turned bloody in the sunset, I ate a whole box of Chocolate Mint Chip Soft Batch Cookies. I slept eleven hours, waking three times in the night: once the moon made everything visible; once it was a shower of warm rain; and once, soon before dawn, I woke up to see the stars.

In the morning, for a moment only, I swam in the too-cold water of the Green River, which was thick with sediment carried down from the north and muddy at the edges. Powell had loved it here, the easiest and most drifting period of a frightening and dangerous

Walking in the bed of Trail Canyon, surrounded by the brutal city blocks of the canyon headlands.

journey. On many days he and his companions would climb high up into the country through which they were passing for the first time. 'Climb the cliffs at the foot of Labyrinth Cañon,' he wrote, 'and you see vast numbers of sharp, angular buttes, and pinnacles and towers, and standing rocks. . . . It seems as if a thousand battles had been fought on the plains below, and on every field the giant heroes had built a monument. . . . The landscape everywhere away from the river is of rock, a pavement of rock with cliffs of rock, tables of rock, plateaus of rock, buttes of rock, ten thousand strangely carved forms; rocks everywhere. . . .'

At a time of day when every pebble casts a shadow, and the hollows in the rocks are still cool from the night before, I walked away from the river, along Upheaval Canyon, towards one of the strangest rock-forms in the whole of the Canyonlands. In the Upheaval Dome the regular sedimentary layers of the Colorado plateau perform a sudden contortion. At some time in the past they seem to have bulged up into a dome about a mile wide, surrounded by a circular depression, like the curving-up brim around a bowler hat. No one knows exactly what happened here but it may be one of two things: either a plug of buoyant but deep-lying salt, finding a structural weakness in the rocks above, has pushed them up into

Looking back down into Syncline Valley to the trench of the Green River.

a dome; or this is the remains of one of the largest meteor-impacts ever experienced on earth. The suggestion is that this broken bubble is no more than the basement of a crater from a catastrophe which may have occurred when the rocks were over a mile higher. Crawl around inside it now; it's like walking into a wound.

The way out of Upheaval Canyon is steep and hot, but every step higher reveals the width of the country which you have been buried inside for two days, a layering of canyons, buttes and distantly snowy mountains. I cannot conceive of ever wanting to own or put my name across any part of a place like this. What can have been Ernie's or Bobby's or Pete's motivation? A desperate absence of anywhere preferable? Or simply the American love of the wild and the extreme, of a place as unearthly as the earth can get? Or, perhaps more simply than that, the pleasures of sleeping, exhausted, flat on one's back, looking up at desert skies, of waking to the cool of a desert morning? It is probably not worth asking anyone these questions in the National Park Service Picnic Place that you find on the road at the top of the canyon. They will think you, without exactly saying so, as they did me, a little over-exposed to the place which they too have come to have see, at least between the Bud and the burgers.

Distances in miles *Alcove Spring Trailhead to Alcove Spring 0.6; to Zeus and Moses 4.7; to mouth of the Big Draw 1.6; to Upheaval Bottom 4.6; to bank of Green River 0.8; to Syncline Valley 3.4; to centre of Upheaval Dome 1.7; back to Syncline Valley 1.7; to National Park Picnic Area 2.9; to Alcove Spring Trailhead 1.0.*

Map *United States Geological Survey* Canyonlands National Park and Vicinity, *one inch to the mile, available at Visitor Centers or Map World, Salt Lake City.*

Books The Cañons of the Colorado, *1981 reprint of Major Powell's account of his 1869 voyage.* Don Baars, Canyonlands Country, *1989, a geological guide.*

Equipment *The most important piece of equipment is a water bottle. The park rangers say that you need a gallon a person a day, which is heavy to carry, but is necessary during the summer when temperatures here can reach 110°F. For the cooler spring and autumn (70s, 80s) you may not need quite so much water. A sun hat is important and some insect repellent. At night temperatures can fall to the 20s in the spring and autumn, 50s in the summer. You will need some waterproofs against late afternoon and evening thunder showers. Campfires are not allowed in the park and so you must take your own stove if you want to cook anything. It is not necessary to bother with a tent. An emergency space blanket is quite enough.*

9.

An Attempt to Cross
the Isle of Wight

The Needles to Carisbrooke

HAMPSHIRE

This was meant to be a recipe for bliss: Far Too Far Through Lush Pastures. The scheme, rather early one Sunday morning, was to walk the breadth of the Isle of Wight in a single day, from the Needles to Bembridge, well over thirty miles. It did not work out that way.

At the western end of the island there is a car park at Alum Bay, next to the cable car and the shops selling bottles filled with the famous coloured sands – not only bottles, but glass cats, glass presidents and glass nudes (in which the sands, intriguingly, model the tones of the female form).

Map in hand, no luggage, make for the western end, where the Isle of Wight comes to its unorthodontic conclusion in the chalk stacks of the Needles. Everything about them confirms what you have ever read about plaque. A quick look at their crumbling is enough – you will be in a hurry. Turn east along the chalk spine that runs ahead for as many miles as you can see. It is the best chalk walk in the country, used but not over-used, a continuous rolling whaleback of downland, where violets and scabious grow in the turf, and wrens are pulled back and forth by the sea winds. The grass, extraordinarily, is covered in lumps of chalk, like a scattering of fossil snow. How do these lumps get here? Is it sheep that pull them out of the one or two rough patches? Or does the wind somehow pluck them out of the cliff face itself?

Past the tall granite memorial to Tennyson on Tennyson Down and then down (running) to Freshwater Bay (a café with the unmistakable holiday smell of motorbike oil and hot children). Quickly on, up Afton Down, where the path goes through the middle of the Freshwater Bay golf course. A hint of the cravat, of the Happy Life – 'I told him he wouldn't get tax relief on it after 5 April, but you know what the young are like'; of the peculiarly bitter humiliations of the game – 'He changed his putter last summer and, you know, his game has never really recovered, but then there was all that business about his wife finding out and Rosemary had to leave –

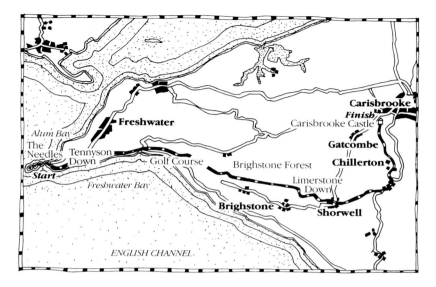

quite a mess in the end'; and of many Bronze Age funerary barrows, marking the line of this ancient ridgeway, all of them now shaved smooth, acting as the oldest golf hazards in the world.

It is a wonderful high path, with the Channel luminous to one side and the Solent full of yachts on the other; I sat down for a moment to look at them both.

Move on, at the peak of your form, socks still springy, lunch inviting, down, up and down over this incomparable chalk – there is no doubt this is bliss – usually out on the open turf, but at one point on the edge of Brighstone forest in a little shaded, gravelly lane where the banks are decorated with hart's tongue fern, primroses and, when I was there the other day, a pair of knickers, hung carefully on a thorn bush, with other scattered testimony of summer nights.

From Limerstone Down, a path (which takes some finding) drops to Shorwell and its pub, the Crown, twelve miles out from Alum Bay. Put your feet in the stream in the pub garden and the pet trout will nibble them.

How is your resolve? Fisherman's pie and a pint of cider are all very well, but when you get up from lunch there is a hint (I am assuming, uncharitably, that you are in as appalling a state as I am), just a hint of that denied, colonizing fear of the one thing you do not need: the blown gasket. You will ignore it, examine the early and pretty spire of Shorwell church and the cowslips in the graveyard, set out along the baby ridgeway east towards Chillerton, watch the

The Needles, where the intention to cross the whole island was quite firm.

hang-gliders avoiding the TV mast on Chillerton Down, thread your way through Chillerton village, and then on along narrow field paths towards Gatcombe, all the time developing a blindness to the acres of map that still separate you from Bembridge.

Just outside the gate into Gatcombe churchyard, there is a bench dedicated to the memory of a Mabel Shaw. It overlooks a dry and rounded valley in the chalk, and is just under six feet long. There, I have to admit it, with the pale purple-grey of Gatcombe church beside me and the sunshine coming through the still bare branches of the beech trees, I lay down and in that drugged and oozy drowsiness that comes from going too far too fast, I fell fast asleep. For three and a half hours.

That was the end of any trans-island schemes. I looked in the church, where there are two marvellous effigies – one wooden, of a crusader; the other alabaster, of a young man killed at Gallipoli, both laid out, supine and easy, with their legs crossed at the ankles.

I walked a couple of miles north in the evening, towards Carisbrooke. A lady from Newport was going the same way. I told her what my coast-to-coast plan had been, expecting some sort of commiseration. 'Oh yes,' she said, 'that's a nice ramble. Jim did it a couple of months ago.'

'And how old is Jim?' I asked.

ABOVE *The Crown Inn at Shorwell. Too much lunch here and things may start to slide downhill.*

BELOW *Carisbrooke Castle, one of the daintiest fortresses in the country.*

'Twelve.'

Carisbrooke is one of the prettiest castles, with low lichened-grey walls and a café. Nothing much has happened there since the imprisonment and attempted escape of Charles I in 1648. He had not measured the windows properly and got stuck between the bars. Jim would probably have done better there too.

> **Distances in miles** *Alum Bay to the Needles 1.1; to Freshwater Bay 3.5; to Shorwell 7.5; to Gatcombe church 4.8; to Carisbrooke Castle 2.1.*
>
> **Map** OS *1:50,000, sheet 196, Isle of Wight.*

10.

In the Ancient Landscape

Hatfield Forest

ESSEX

The more that landscape historians look at what actually happened to the ancient English countryside, the more it seems that, between the Iron Age and the nineteenth century, nothing very much happened to it at all. It is not really true, as one writer after another has claimed, that each new age has changed the landscape to meet its own needs.

As scholars are starting to discover, before the deep transformations and collective oblivion of the twentieth century, much of rural England probably looked and worked as it had done for thousands of years. It is not, as is often said, a palimpsest, a parchment from which one text has been rubbed away so that another can be written over it. It seems likely that the landscape is a single document on which marks have been made over a very long period. Extras have been added in the margins or between the lines, changing a word here and there, but almost never a whole paragraph. The changes have not removed what went before, but have simply complicated it, sustained it and enriched it.

Because the current orthodoxy runs so strongly in the other direction (ie, people have always been transforming the landscape; modern changes are only shocking because they are so recent), it takes a moment to grasp this. But what it means is that as you walk through the older landscapes of England (essentially not eighteenth and nineteenth-century enclosures), what you are witnessing is as dazzling and complete a piece of historical reality as you can ever hope to find. Hollywood has nothing on a muddy afternoon in Essex, where the passage of historical time folds up like a fan.

What you see around you is not the last in a series of historical scenes stretching into the original oblivion, gradually getting darker and more indistinct. Not at all. This, what you have in front of your eyes, here and now, at least in its essentials, is one of the earliest scenes of all.

In some places, of course, the presence of the ancient past is clearer

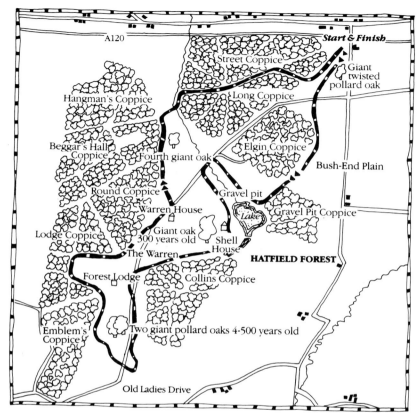

than in others, and Hatfield Forest is one of the best. It is a piece of soggy wood, neat in parts, run loose in others, with plains of grassland in between (some of it spoilt with chemical treatment in the Fifties but now recovering), huge trees and young thickets. These one-and-a-half square miles in north-west Essex were, throughout the seventeenth and eighteenth centuries, the subject of endless legal argument between competing grandees who owned different parts and had rights to different aspects of it. As a result, a mass of records was dredged up by the lawyers on either side, recording all the medieval habits, costs, complaints, difficulties, triumphs and ways of life in the forest and its surroundings.

But Hatfield does not survive only in the records. Every part of a medieval forest is still there in reality: the fallow deer which the royal forest was primarily intended to nurture; the blocks of woodland, where tall timber trees stand over the underwood which, for at least 800 years, have been coppiced, leaving huge spreading stools from which the new shoots spring; the cattle grazing the grassy plains between these woodland coppices; the pollards standing in the plains, from which wood is cut only above the grazing height of cattle, leaving a giant, twisted bole, or *bolling,* for the cows to rub their flanks against; a rabbit warren, with its seventeenth-century warrener's house; and a late medieval forest lodge, placed in the very centre of the forest, positioned with a view to surveying everything that might happen in the plains.

The reason Hatfield is so complete is not because it is an obscure and remote corner of the country: Bishop's Stortford, the M11 and the expanding Stansted airport are all within spitting (and acid rain) distance. Nevertheless (but not on bank holidays), it can be a place of deep and beautiful quiet, especially in the western coppices, where the old cut stools of coppiced oakwood, some of them at least as ancient as Robert the Bruce, one of the early lords of the forest, jut out like rounded and buffeted corals in the ragged woodland surrounding them.

This is not a place for marching determinedly from point to point. The forest is a profoundly conservative place, the creation of slowness, of endless repetition, of a careful interfolding of the demands of trees, deer, men and their cattle, a place which shares the nature of the trees it harbours – long-lasting, immobile and beautiful. You should come here not to walk but to *moon,* to spend whole days with your hands in your pockets and no goal in view.

And in this, luckily, you will have a wonderful guide. Oliver Rackham, a don at Corpus Christi in Cambridge, has just written a brilliant and iconoclastic book on Hatfield, *The Last Forest.* It is the result of twenty years' research, in which every tree is looked at, every management practice considered, every part of the dynamic equilibrium of a working forest given its due.

It is a long and immensely detailed book – and that is its point: only in the exactness of the specific detail can the nature of a rich historical landscape be properly known. What the author reveals is not only the workings of a medieval social and biological system in pretty much its original order, but the unique survival in England of a way of life which runs deep in human nature throughout the world – the system of wood-pasture found in Scandinavia, Finland,

Pollards, some split to the root, stand about on the 'plains' between the blocks of coppiced woodland. The young shoots on the head of a pollard are too high for cattle to eat them.

the Alps and the Apennines, Greece and on into the Himalayas. Nor is its extent only geographical.

'Our Neolithic ancestors,' Dr Rackham says, springing a characteristic surprise, 'might well find themselves at home here' (here being half a mile from the end of Stansted runway, in a landscape which the men of medieval Essex would have thought their own).

You can walk anywhere you like in the forest, but do at least make sure that in your mooning here and there you get to see the following:

BUSH-END PLAIN   This used to be a coppice, but all that is left are the old oak and maple pollards standing above the cow pasture. Just at the eastern corner of Street Coppice is a particularly splendid pollard oak, its entire body twisted into a giant corkscrew. At the southern end of the plain, near Gravel Pit Coppice, are a series of pollard hornbeams, part of the National Trust's recent revival of this practice in the forest.

LAKE   Created by the owners of the forest, the Houblon family, in the eighteenth century as part of a scheme to turn what Rackham calls 'a first-rate medieval forest into a fourth-rate country park'. Enormous fish are pulled from its waters. This is the most visited part of the entire forest.

SHELL HOUSE   A pretty tea-room built by the Houblons in the 1740s, covered in flints and shells. Just outside it stands the largest tree in the forest today – an oak which is probably about 300 years old and, Rackham reckons, comprising about 800 cubic feet of timber. It is in the prime of life and will live, he says, to become one of the biggest oaks in England.

FOREST LODGE   The seventeenth-century exterior conceals a medieval core. Rackham explains how there might once have been a lookout tower attached to this house, perhaps built in the sixteenth century, from which ceremonial hunts might have been viewed (unlikely) or where foresters could keep an eye on things.

GIANT POLLARDS   South of Forest Lodge, a pair of massive oak trees are tucked just inside the edge of the scrubland growing up on what used to be open grassland plain. You can climb up into the crook of one of them, from which six branches, each as big as a fair-size oak tree, splay out like a giant hand.

LODGE COPPICE   Here is the quietest and most remote corner of the forest, crowded with Arthur (rather than Oliver) Rackhamesque stools of coppiced oak, cut and recut for many centuries, distorted into bulbous grotesqueries.

WARREN HOUSE   A little seventeenth century cottage sits next to the lumpy 'pillow mounds' of the warren, built so that the rabbits

Oliver Rackham standing in one of the pair of giant pollard oaks between Emblem's and Collin's Coppices.

would burrow into them. Rabbits were kept for the sweetness of their flesh. Huge chestnuts now grow all over the mounds.

BEGGAR'S HALL COPPICE Portingbury Rings is the name given to a few lumps in the wood which may perhaps be the remains of an Iron Age farm, but no one is sure. More interestingly, on the eastern edge of the coppice, there is another of the forest's giant oaks, slashed with lightning down one side and with a girth at breast height of twenty feet. It might be 300 or 400 years old.

LONG COPPICE The National Trust has recently coppiced this piece of woodland. Here you can see exactly the way in which Hatfield Forest has been maintained for the last 800 years.

The Shell House, built in the 1740s next to the lake, was part of the mid-eighteenth-century scheme to convert the forest into a pleasure-landscape. For night-time feasts, the branches of this oak tree were hung with lanterns.

Maps OS *1:25,000* TL 41/51 (*Harlow North and Hatfield Heath*); TL 42/52 (*Bishop's Stortford and Stansted Airport*).

Book *Oliver Rackham* The Last Forest (*Dent, 1989*).

11.

Up Manhattan

New York

Where Manhattan comes to its artificial point in Battery Park, built out into the bay after decades of accumulating rubbish from the foundations of buildings to the north, the view is ecstatic – Brooklyn across the water, Liberty on her island, the sun on the oilers moving out to the Narrows and the Atlantic beyond them. Here the first Dutch settlers in New Amsterdam landed from Europe, and from here they returned. It was known as the Weeping Quay, named after its twin in Holland.

Turn north to the cliff of the business district. It is like an English port town – Chichester, Woodbridge or Whitby – grown big on itself, a freak baby, weighing twenty stone, a little thing thick with elephantiasis, the bloated members pinned to a fragile structure of winding, narrow streets. Trinity Church at the head of Wall Street, facing the Bank of Tokyo and the Irving Trust Co, sits here as a black little grandmother dwarfed by her shining progeny.

North of the money belt, moving up Nassau Street, there is a sudden growth of messy shops, selling hiking gear, fishing tackle and bras reduced by twenty per cent. On the street in front of the vent, where the steak-flavoured air is blown out from the restaurant kitchen at passing feet, a man lies whispering about his children and the pencils he has for sale.

For a city so famous for its divisions, there is a curiously easy slurring of categories as you pass from big business to marginal enterprise and on to City Hall, the courts and government offices. Here is one great pleasure of New York: sliding by, the Los Angeles sensation on foot, the sidewalk as a freeway. . . .

Up Centre Street, along the fringe of Chinatown, and then cutting over by Lafayette to the edge of SoHo on Broadway, the girls are all in black, their shoes are patent, stick-on rubber on the sole, and their hair is designer-messy. The men's necks are shaved up to their

Urban canyons off Fifth Avenue.

BELOW *The moral drama of the city enacted on its streets every day, where the homeless and the hungry are canny enough to choose the most poignant places at which to beg.*

heads so that if you walk behind them you can see the tendons of the neck moving under the grey screen of bristle on skin. SoHo is zoned for 'Art'.

And then, sweetly, most magical of all, the glutinous smell of dry-cleaning fluid, blown in an invisible flag across the sidewalk on the corner of Mercer and Bleeker, on the edge of the Village. One block on, a blind man, still self-conscious of his look in clothes he cannot see, is led across the ragged intersections by his guide dog.

On these streets – given a furry look by the fire escapes which half hide and half express the buildings on which they grow like stubble – sheltering under some plastic sheeting torn from the walls of a building site behind him, a derelict lies whispering: 'Please, please, feed me.' He leans like a Roman at dinner, one elbow on the pavement, the other crooked out towards the passers-by.

You reach Washington Square and move up the blanded-out lower reaches of Fifth Avenue, where a woman – she's in account management, with prophetic eyes and a seductive, drawn-out Southern drawl – is overseeing the shooting of a commercial. For the ad, well-dressed young women are drinking tea and smearing

ABOVE *Big is rich: one pole of the New York vision of itself — the car as the horizontal skyscraper.*

the backs of their hands across their lips afterwards. The idea, she says, is to target coffee, because coffee is 'vulnerable'.

Sliding along, west of Fifth and going north through the flower shops, the potted gardens on the sidewalks (between Broadway and Seventh around 28th Street) and then the Garment District and the sweatshops with Korean signs hanging out into the street (all through here up to 40th Street), you reach the porn movie cinemas on Eighth Avenue (X X Xotic X X Xcessive X X Xtravaganzas).

I had lunch at Jean Lafitte on 68 West 58th Street. It was delicious. A place where authors, wearing consciously ragged jeans and shirts made sweaty by real life, smile to their lipsticked agents smiling across at them, and joke about the age of boyfriends and the problem of always repeating one's father in the boyfriends one chooses. The agents order the boys lobster because that's what they deserve. Their other acquaintances speak bad French to the waiter from Milwaukee, who speaks bad French back until, without laughing, the French

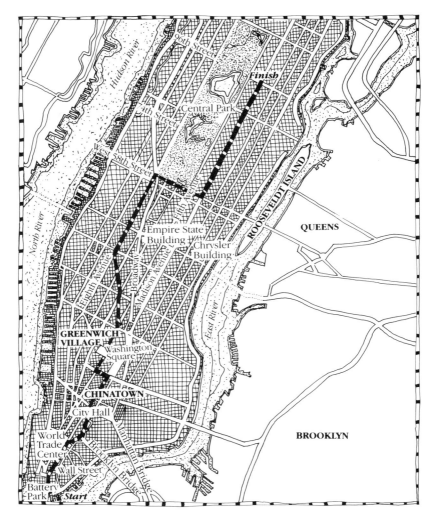

breaks down and one asks of the other. 'What's the soup anyway?' The answer, 'French onion,' is also delivered without laughter. And mid-conversation the young woman leans away towards some passers-by: 'Nice sale.' They smile backwards as they pass with a sideways flick of the head – meaning yes – because yesterday they sold a treatment (thirty pages, all grit) on a sequel to Gone with the Wind for $4.94m. That translates to $494,000 for them.

'What I find difficult to understand,' you hear across the room, 'is the glut of babies on the menus this spring.' And he's right. If it's not babies, it's withered. Or both. Baby-rabbit ears gathered from the flower-strewn meadows of upstate Quebec, withered in an antique cognac flame and laid on a coronet of faded spinach crests. Or coffee.

And then on and out to the blazing sunshine in this town where you can call a nightclub Siberia, Heartbreak, King Tut's Wa-Wa Hut, or Downtown Beirut, as if these things were not part of the world they live in, and on this sunlit, busy afternoon the great skyscraping avenues look glamorous in their huge and shadowed darkness.

Across Fifth Avenue to Madison, you find the over-whitened whiteness of New York skins and those women in their shouldered suits with exaggerated beautiful calves that emerge tailored from below the tailoring. Block after block something worried me. There was something almost spookily coherent about the street. What lay behind this moneyed coherence north of 60th Street? And then I realized: it is the only place in the world where the people look like shops. Not like the mannequins or the clothes on display in the shops, but like the shops themselves. The fashion ideal of Madison Avenue is plate-glass sunglasses, a suit that looks as much as possible like wipe-down tiling and tone-in grout, the face plastered white, the 'ambience', as they might say in Jean Lafitte, exuding wealth despite every effort to deny it.

On 74th and Madison there was grass for sale, mini-prairies in little black pots. On 77th, a Henry Moore shop, the crusty bread shop, the P.S.-I-Love-You shop, and the do-your-bedroom-out-in-brass-and-broderie-anglaise-because-you'll-feel-better shop.

At the end, north of 96th Street, it is not Madison that darkens but the cross-streets which empty and roughen, which lose the shine, and are not made-up. At this junction at last is the encroaching air, coming up on the flank, of suppression, anger and failure. Look back at that lit slot to the south, then bring your eyes lower and down to the street and see the self-sufficiency of prosperous New York mixed with the occasionally flaccid face of the Upper East Side inheritance millionaire. He wears flat soft shoes, as wide as cars, a wide-fringed tassel laid across them, and has that near-whine present in his watery voice of the never-anything-but-joking upper-class American rich. Standing at the edge of Harlem, in the oily dusk, you will hear the two rhythms of this city, each distinct, each hardly connected with the other: on top, hard, quick, excitable, and vicious, the rhythm of money; below, deeper, slower, scarcely heard unless you listen for it, seeping out like the plumes of steam from the pores in the road, the undertones of sorrow.

12.

Seaside Grace
and Georgian Favour

Weymouth

DORSET

As everyone, I'm sure, knows by now, 1789 was the year of one of
the most significant events in history: George III's first swim. He
was completely mad. The court was in despair, the Prince of Wales
disgusting, the queen hysterical, and the French republican. There
was only one thing for it: royal swimming.

On the Dorset coast, just outside the ancient and decrepit twin
towns of Melcombe Regis and Weymouth, the king's brother, the
Duke of Gloucester, had a smallish holiday house. This was to be
the spot where the English crown could be returned to full health,
and where the custom of the seaside holiday would be confirmed as
the right and proper thing to do.

The town was rigid with excitement. How could it not be when
it was about to strike the eighteenth-century equivalent of oil?
Workmen were down from London, refurbishing streets and houses;
the whole town had gone mad on decorations, with the golden motto
'God Save the King' painted up on shops and bathing machines, on
the hats of children and sailors, and on great *girdles* around the bellies
of the bathing-women.

All morning on 30 June 1789, and half of the afternoon, the
mayor, aldermen and common council waited on the outskirts of the
town, their colours flying and the town band repeatedly practising
the national anthem. At four o'clock the royal party arrived. The
men-of-war lying in Weymouth Bay fired a salute. There were flags
everywhere. It was the happiest moment in the history of the world.

The court looked only mildly patronizing, the king quite well.
But what did he think? The mayor and common council strained to
hear his verdict. The ugliest man ever to have sat on the English
throne looked at the bay. He paused a moment and 'in terms of
real satisfaction' uttered the most valuable sentence ever heard in
Weymouth: 'I never enjoyed a sight so pleasing.' It was going to be
a bonanza.

Go to Weymouth today, and what you find is the most perfect

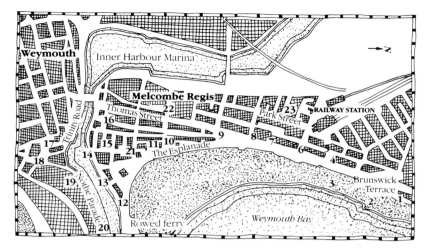

Brunswick Terrace: the mixture of strict decorum and a hint of bow-fronted playfulness which is Georgian seaside architecture at its best.

mixture of the two contradictory things the English seaside does better than any other: a real Georgian grace – billowy architecture of the best kind, streets and statues on holiday – on the most beautiful bay in the country. And, though Weymouth won't like this much, a rather slummy quality, the sheer tat that has gathered around the Georgian streets, with none of that smartened-upness which has afflicted almost every small town in southern England.

Walk along the great curve of the Esplanade and you will find in its raw state, un-pre-packaged, the best seaside town in England, which had its short and glorious royal period (it was over by 1805) and which ever since has been enjoying a long and rather casual downward slide from its peak of fashionability.

Start at the northern end, at Brunswick Terrace **1** (see map p. 73), finished in 1827, scalloped into a string of shallow bay windows, now a succession of baby hotels. On past the remains of the 1930s pier bandstand **2**, the only interruption to the beautiful sands. The

LEFT *The pre-Georgian townscape of the harbour, the fishing fleet deep inside it, the yachts further out.*

BELOW *The Jubilee Clock tower on the Esplanade, put up in 1887 – a bauble of late Victorian jollity set against the level brows of the earlier terraces.*

Esplanade swings away ahead of you. There are some very good trampolines on the sand here **3**, which you can rent for a quick bounce or two. Past the terrace known as Belvidere **4**, only completed in the 1850s. Then cut down to the back of Royal Crescent into Crescent Street **5** where you can find some of the very pretty second-rank Georgian houses, built for slightly poorer holidaymakers, one street away from the sands.

Return to the Esplanade at King Street **6** where Weymouth has taken it upon itself to build an underpass (!). You only have to ask the question: 'What about the underpass then?' in any Weymouth pub and you're the hero for the night.

On along the Esplanade, past the Victorian extravaganza of the Royal Hotel **7** which is now owned by a bus company from Wigan, and where on Thursdays you can attend a *thé dansant*. A little further on is the old Gloucester Hotel **8**, the house where the king stayed.

Almost next to the Gloucester, slapped into a series of late eighteenth-century houses, are Kentucky Bingo Hall and Slotsafun amusement arcade. The Coin-o-matix is good. With your winnings, walk on past the polychrome statue of George III **9**, erected in 1809 as it says 'by the *grateful* inhabitants', to the best pub in Weymouth, The Town Crier **10**, run by Doris Eastwood, the splendid and statuesque town crier herself. Very good jazz here in season, in a building which was originally Harvey's Card and Assembly Rooms. Next **11** the most flamboyant public convenience in the country, occupying the ground floor of a wonderful miniature Renaissance château built as a bank in 1883 with apricot brick and cream stone facings.

At the end of the Esplanade, you turn the corner of the pretty Devonshire Buildings **12** and enter the world of Weymouth before 1789 – the harbour. Gin-thick yachts **13** line up here, followed by the rawer shell-fishing boats **14**. The slightly basic nightclub Verdi's **15** is in Maiden Street, where one can witness a string of fascinating holidaymaker/local girl encounters, rarely very successful.

On past the very grand Guildhall **16** in St Edmund Street, put up by Melcombe Regis in what had been the heart of the medieval town before the holiday boom but now seems to be the neglected middle of the place. Then over the bridge to the other of the twin towns, Old Weymouth itself. The atmosphere is quite different here, less flash, more villagey. Visit the sixteenth-century house in Trinity Road **17** which is run by the Civic Society and houses some fascinating objects, and then walk past the big brick Devenish Brewery in Hope Square **18**, closed down now, and past the boatyard **19**, which has certainly been working here since the fifteenth century. Continue all the way along the southern edge of the harbour to the rowing boat ferry **20** which takes you back on to the Melcombe side.

The last part of the walk is more back-streety. Along the rather nooky St Albans Street **21**, charming but thick with cafés etc, and then over to the west side of town, which is being redeveloped into a monster shopping centre **22**, which involves the demolition and façading of various eighteenth-century buildings. Someone in Weymouth borough council described the new scheme to me as ersatz fifteenth-century Florentine.

Finally, make your way to Park Street **23**, an almost untampered-with piece of early nineteenth-century working-class town planning, where you will find boxing videos on in the pubs and an utterly sympathetic street scene, the best of small-town England. From here you can easily make your way back to your starting-point on Brunswick Terrace.

13.

The Shifting Island

Hatteras

NORTH CAROLINA

You can't see America from Hatteras. The coast of North Carolina is over the western horizon from the island, beyond the waters of Pamlico Sound, twenty-six miles of smooth lagoon which separates the sand and salt marsh of the barrier islands from the continental United States. When the Italian navigator Giovanni di Varrazzano came here in the 1520s, he thought Hatteras was all there was to America and that the Sound was the ocean that stretched from here to Japan. He didn't bother to look any further.

Hatteras is still one of the most perfect and least developed of all the barrier islands that rim the Atlantic from Maine to Texas. It is little more than a shoal made good, never more than thirty feet high, sometimes a mile or two wide, often a quarter of that, and to walk down it for a day or two is like walking the deck of a ship at sea. Every phase and shift in the weather registers on your skin; the wind is constant; the surf and spray on the ocean side beat against you as if against a hull.

'Catching some Zs?' the man said to me. His hat said 'I'd rather be fishin' on the Outer Banks.' I was indeed asleep in my sleeping bag on a bed of pine needles at the southern end of Bodie Island waiting for the day to get a little older. 'You've got to be discreet if you want to sleep out,' he said. He was an old man, just nosing around seeing what was what, and he didn't speak with any recognizable American accent. It was a more clotted, round-vowelled thing, which said 'Hoi!' instead of 'Hi!' and is claimed by some to be the remnants of Elizabethan English. Sir Walter Ralegh's first English colony on Roanoke Island just to the north of here disappeared without trace in 1590. When the next Englishmen came to the place there was no sign of death, only the deserted and broken houses. The word CROATOANS, the name of the people who lived on Hatteras at the time, was carved on a post at the entrance to the colony. A century later there were reports of some light-skinned, pale-eyed people living among the Indians on the island, but the fate of the colony,

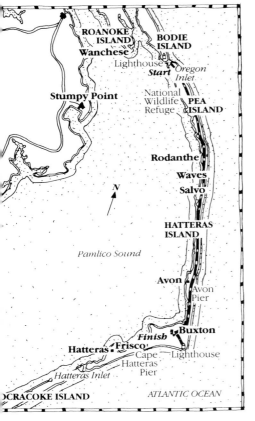

of these first English Americans who might perhaps have joined in with the people they found there, remains a mystery. I asked the man about Elizabethan English. Yes, he'd heard that too, but he couldn't rightly say. 'I don't know how they spoke in them days.'

Hatteras is divided from Bodie Island and the other barrier islands to the north by the dangerous and broken waters of the Oregon Inlet, a mile-wide breach in the sand-barrier smashed through by a hurricane in 1846. This perforation and splitting of the islands happens constantly, at least on the scale of geological time. Holes are broken through by storms; others migrate, as Oregon Inlet itself has done, many miles to the south; still others open and then as quickly close again.

A beautiful clean bridge, carrying State Highway 12 south on to Hatteras, now crosses the inlet, arching in its centre to allow the passage of ships underneath. A dredger works here every stormless day of the year, attempting to keep the channel free of the mountains of sand dragged down by the longshore drift from the north. The dredger can't keep up and big stone jetties are under construction on both sides to hold the sand away from the channel. But talk to anyone on the island about this or any other attempt to still the vast natural movements of current and sand on the Outer Banks and you will get the same head-shaking reply. This island is nothing fixed. It is inexorably on the move; the whole place is moving west towards America. It has transience, shiftingness, built into its very existence. No one is quite sure about their origins, but these sands may have begun as the deltas of continental river systems from a time when the sea was much lower during the Ice Age. As the sea has risen it has pushed them back up the continental shelf towards the present land mass. The ocean is a broom, the islands the dust in front of it. At least some of the real estate agents on the island are alert to this. Houses well back from the beach now are sold on the basis of 'Ocean Front property by the turn of the century'. Even erosion can turn a buck.

Beyond the bridge and the coast guard station, which has been temporarily abandoned because salt water has invaded its wells, you are out on to Hatteras Island, the pure thing. Since 1936 it has been part of America's first National Seashore and since 1952 has been managed by rangers and coastal ecologists as a national park. The control is discreet. Cut down on to the Atlantic beach, across the dunes, and the illusion is there, anyway, that this is not a protected place but one that has been simply uninterfered with. It's a naked strand, a runway of a beach, running two or more days ahead of you without a break, a strip of desert a hundred yards wide and forty miles long. The only way to walk it is a slow and steady rhythm that wheels up the miles like a man rolling in a tape measure. After an hour or two it becomes a sort of metronomic dream, a version of oblivion with a regular beat, in which the sun shines into your eyes and the sun beats on to your cheek and the great walls of the Atlantic swell break half a mile or more out at sea, their surf and wash running into the shore in a chaos of frothed water. These shores with their off-lying shoals have been known for centuries as the Graveyard of the Atlantic, as ship after ship has been blown on to them and the crew drowned. The Hatteras Coast Guard has long been famous for its rescues through this wide and destructive surf. There is an unofficial motto: 'The rule book says you have to go out. It don't say you have to come back.'

Three miles down the beach you should come back across the dunes to the Pea Island Wildlife Refuge, a carefully monitored bit of wetland, half artificial and half natural, where many northern birds over-winter and where, on the March day I was there, a solitary snow-goose floated in a black and reedy pond.

But this is not a walk for incidents or arrivals; it is about continuity, the American length of things. Such a beach would be inconceivable in Europe. There is nothing tight or contained about it. It is sheer extent. You could see the whole history of America – its amazement at the natural wonders of the new world; its extraordinary indifference to its desecration of them – as the simple product of minds used to the constraints of Europe meeting this sort of unconstraint, the sheer extravagance of natural form, the hugeness of gesture which makes up America.

Then, as you are sliding off down the beach towards Rodanthe, fifteen miles down the island from Oregon Inlet, something else starts to happen. Given the sheer scale of the edge along which you are walking – the ocean meets the first outlier of the continent – your focus shifts to much smaller things. In the dunes the tips of the salt grass, bending over and jiggled by the wind, etch palmetto-fan patterns in the sand around their stems. The tracks of a ghost-crab, sewn over the surface of the dune like a meandering hem, disappear into a miniature cave, the miniature heap of excavated sand slithering down the dune below it. In the line of storm-driven wrack, high on the beach, the half-rotted body of a bottle-nose dolphin lies part-drifted into the sand. There is a skin of blue fungus on the exposed bone and, around the rigid dark body of the animal, the patterning of gulls' feet, where they have been standing at a steak bar, pecking at the flesh. Little parties of sanderlings run back and forth in the wash like dealers on the exchange floor, poking into the sand and gravel turned up by the latest waves. Dark pelicans almost at the northern limit of their range coast over the sands, their heads screwed back into their bodies, and then veer out to sea, plunging into it with abandon for fish.

Then, as you trudge along, yard after yard, hour after hour, there are the shells: the most beautiful charcoal-grey scallops and conches, most of them drilled by the birds for the flesh inside, others eaten away by the rubbing of the sea, their smooth helical structures inside revealed like a diagram of growth by a Renaissance scientist. But you are not the first person to notice the beauty of these things. A few miles short of Rodanthe a washed-up tree has been stood upright in the sand and its stubbed worn-away branches hung with these half-open shells, calcium structures that look like skulls, the dried fruit on dried-out branches.

In the spray-haze the first houses of Rodanthe appear like towers in the mist. Eventually you reach them, set back behind the dunes on thirty-foot stilts, lifted above the overwash. The flood waters can come either from the ocean, when a north-easterly drives the water through the dunes, or from the Sound, as happened last in 1985, when Hurricane Gloria moved north just west of the island, first sucking the fishing harbours dry and then releasing the stack of water it had built up in the head of the Sound in a tidal wave that poured over the island and back into the Atlantic. The carcases of flounder and pike were found by the returning residents strewn around the foot of the houses. The place, for a moment anyway, had been awash with the element that dominates it. The people of

The view from Hatteras lighthouse down the narrow island strip towards Avon and beyond.

Rodanthe and Avon were worried for days that with the rise in the water-table the bodies of their dead would begin to float up out of the graves.

Rodanthe, particularly out of season before the influx of summer fishermen arrive, feels like the back of beyond. The air in the Sand Dollar is thick with testosterone. 'You didn't heat that darlin',' the barmaid is told and someone nips her butt. One fisherman is just back from Key West. 'Went for two weeks, stayed three years. And I found out something. To get anywhere in that place you have to be one of three things – gay, Greek or groovy.' 'I knew that the day I got there,' he is told by a man who hasn't left Hatteras in a decade, where none of the three phenomena in question has ever been sighted. Everyone slugs at the Coors. This is de-regulation, I'm-my-own-man America, where the general mess of Rodanthe – the stacks of rotting cars, the absence of anything like a zoning law – is seen as evidence of freedom. It's Wyoming-by-the-Sea.

The gale came in at night from the north-east. A drenching wall of wind and rain beat over the island all day as I walked to the southern point. You could watch the beach steepening as the Atlantic tore at its outer edge, carrying truck-loads of sand down towards the cape. The sea, from its green planktony blue of the day before,

The lighthouse at Cape Hatteras, a landmark for shipping on a dangerous coast and the end of the walk.

had turned black. Hatteras was not friendly. The rain-soaked sand clogged each step. As I write this, the tendons in my calves are still sore from the day-long pulling of the sand. In the edge of the surf a huge creature, twenty feet from nose to tail, lay dead, rolling to and fro. It was a beak-nosed whale, its body complete and glistening. Often enough these mammals are washed up on the Hatteras shore. The Rangers report them and biologists from the Smithsonian come down to remove their stomachs, which are analysed back in Washington, before the remains are buried under the sand. Further on a sun-fish lay beached on the berm, its rectangular but round-cornered body the shape of breakfast table, about six feet long and four wide. No one is quite sure how these deep ocean fish end up on the beach, but it is perhaps to do with the complex meeting of currents that occurs offshore. From the north the Cold Shelf Current sidles down the edge of America, bringing waters that began in the Arctic. Further out, but no more than twelve miles east of Cape Hatteras, where the continental shelf drops away to the depths of the central Atlantic, the Gulf Stream moves north in an eddying river of tropical water, still seventy degrees Fahrenheit this far north, bringing marlin and other billfish within reach of day excursions from the Hatteras ports. With a lull in the storm, and the sky clearing for a moment, one can see the heavy band of warm clouds on the horizon, the wet warmth of the Gulf Stream rising into the atmosphere, a bubbly white stripe across the planet which can be seen from space.

But the storm returns, heavier and blacker than before, and the tops of the seas are whipped away like froth off beer. The beach is coated with white bubbly scum, building up in ponds and ridges on the sand. Muddled in with the froth pools are lumps – of all things – of *peat*. This alien, un-marine thing is some of the best evidence that the island is on the move westwards. These lumps are the remains of an acid peat bog which a few centuries ago gathered on the Sound side of the island. Over the years Hatteras has simply rolled across its former self. What was the Sound shore now meets the Atlantic.

It was the kind of weather, drenching, freezing, open Atlantic weather, the body leant sideways into the wind as if running your shoulder against the line of a wall, in which all you can think of is things you once did, things you might have done better. For some shelter, I crossed over the dunes, which are in fact semi-artificial barriers set up in the past few decades in an attempt – now abandoned – to stop the movement westwards. The wind drops in their lee and you walk for miles over a kind of salty lawn, the barrier flat, where salt meadow cordgrass and bright lichens mat together over the sand, a stabilizing skin. Further west, a thicket of myrtles and briars is almost impenetrable. In the occasional pond a heron or snowy egret pokes and plunges in the knee-deep water. Here and there an opening in the thicket gives way to the shores of the Sound, where the foetid mud stinks and the waters of the lagoon are darkened with catspaws breaking off the island.

I came to Avon and had lunch in the Froggy Dog. The conversation was of real estate and diets. An army vicar told me to go to church sometimes and was pleased that the value of his property had risen tenfold in fifteen years. He would have passed to a better place before the ocean reached his house.

On and on, a broad reach along the wind, seven miles to the light. I felt I had been at sea all day, battened down, the hatches shut against the weather. Pairs of duck beat straight into the wind, their air-speed almost nil. I was looking for the lighthouse many miles before I reached it. It is 208 feet high, the tallest in the United States, and perhaps the most famous. It is painted in diagonal black and white candy stripes. I thought I saw it but the spray hazed over again, and then it came again and remained this time. It was a grey floating finger, still an hour away, but slowly, increasingly slowly, it approached.

I reached the light, looked briefly up at its giant Victorian pin-prick, the only vertical in a world of horizontals, and collapsed back into a motel in Buxton, which at least had a hot bath. At dinner, there was stuffed flounder on the menu. I ate enough of it until I felt like one.

Distances in miles *Oregon Inlet to Pea Island Wildlife Refuge 3; to Rodanthe 12; to Waves 1; to Salvo 2; to Avon 15; to Buxton 7; to the lighthouse 1; back to Buxton 1.*

Map *It is difficult to get hold of the United States Geological Service maps of the Outer Banks. A usable substitute is a free sheet advertising shops and motels on the island, which you can pick up in many places.*

14.

The Fens

Chatteris to Ely

CAMBRIDGESHIRE

It must be easy to feel frightened living in the Fens. Farmhouses here are usually isolated: it is definitely not the sort of place to surprise someone by coming up on them suddenly. Leaving Chatteris in the Cambridgeshire Fens the other day, I did exactly that. On the map, a white lane leads invitingly north from the town and sets out directly for a farmhouse one mile away across Nightlayer's Fen. The map marks a little bridge at the end of the lane over Forty Foot Drain; you might think nothing could go wrong.

But it can. The track is private. At its end, in the farmhouse, sits the woman who owns both the path and the surrounding field. This is her territory and is not to be infringed. She is angry with people who imagine they can walk where their fancy takes them. The bridge on the map was demolished three years ago and her Dobermans, she says, throw themselves through the plate glass windows at trespassing innocents. It is not worth the risk. To avoid this particular hurdle, start your walk at Curf, where the Chatteris-Wimblington road crosses the Forty Foot Drain.

Straight away you will find all the intriguing elements of the Fens. It is the most controlled landscape in the country but one which breeds anxiety not contentment. Not a weed nor a stone interferes with the sampler-trim planting of the fields; an absolute straightness of drains – this one, the Forty Foot or Vermuyden's, was a key work dug by Sir Cornelius Vermuyden, the great Dutch hydraulic engineer, in 1651; and neat brick farms out in their own in the middle of their flatlands. All this is somehow tense, almost obsessively alert to the orderly.

But there are anomalies, too. The peat has gradually been shrinking away since it was first drained in the seventeenth century. It is disappearing at the rate of about one inch a year, shrivelled by the surface drought and diminished by the Fen 'blows' that pick up the fine tilth soil and carry it out, in dark curtains of dust, to sea.

Much of this ground is now well below sea level. High Water

Springs, the highest tide in the Wash, thirty miles to the northeast, is twenty feet or more above the gravel on which you are now walking. This has its implications for the landscape. Both the Forty Foot and the Sixteen Foot Drains were cut 200 years ago when the land level was much higher. The drains now stand higher than the fields they serve. The shrinking of the peat has left them varicose, standing proud, almost as applied pipes on the skin of the country. Electric pumping stations stand at every

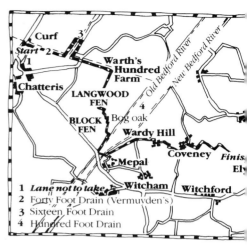

junction, lifting the water from field ditches into subsidiary channels and from there into the main drains. It may be these two elements in the Fenland – the vanishing fertility (in some places the peat has completely gone leaving nothing but sand and clay) and the presence of large bodies of water, as high as the bedroom ceilings in the houses crouched next to them – which make the Fens so quietly threatening.

These fields have virtually nothing to do with bogginess now. Only the occasional flag of a Norfolk reed stands on the side of a bank, missed by the flail cutter, a remnant of the damp-, ague- and eel-ridden landscape that was here before the drainers came. What you are walking through is in effect a Renaissance landscape. What Vermuyden achieved would have been impossible without accurate maps, precise surveying instruments and the sense of encompassing rationality which arrived in this country from Europe in the seventeenth century. Of course, with the passing of time, this strictness of vision has in places settled into a maturer ease. The stretch of Vermuyden's Drain between Hollyhouse and Warth's Hundred Farm is now hidden under a beautiful and dense wood of thorn trees, the drain hidden by their branches, which in early summer is blanketed in white flowers.

Beyond Warth's Hundred Farm you leave Vermuyden's Drain and zigzag down through Langwood and Block Fens towards Mepal. Far away to the east the towers of Ely Cathedral float on the haze. Nearer at hand are the rusting gantries of the now-defunct Block Fen sandpits. The peat disappeared from here many years ago,

Fishing in the Block Fen sandpits.

revealing sand. Now that, too, is worked out and the pits are flooded and you can fish for trout for a daily fee. It comes as no surprise in the Fens to learn that someone out of a secret envy is said to have slipped a *zander* – a monstrous Dutch hybrid of a perch and a pike – into the waters of a nearby lake, where for a while it committed effortless trout genocide until it was found one day washed up on the bank, gorged with its prey.

About half a mile from the sandpits, look carefully in the ditch on the left of the track. There you will see the giant black corpse of a bog oak which is probably 5,000 years old. About sixty feet long and carelessly dumped off the field, it was part of the forest which grew here in the clay valley before the sea level started to rise in about 3000 BC and the trees were killed off by the waterlogging of their roots. The oak collapsed where it had grown; but its wood was preserved by the accumulating layers of peat which have now been pared away to reveal the oak once more. Fen farmers find these trees all the time. Some are accompanied by traces of Neolithic man.

You are now approaching the best part of this walk. It is, in a way, the most paradoxical. Slashed over the middle of these southern Fens, in a running twenty-one-mile-wide double-stripe, is the central mechanism of Vermuyden's drainage scheme: the Old Bedford River, dug in about 1637, and its twin the New Bedford River, or Hundred

On the Hundred Foot Washes.

Foot Drain, dug fifteen years later by 11,000 men. The two rivers run parallel about half a mile apart. When the Fens are in danger of flooding, large quantities of water are allowed to spill over into the strip of land between the two rivers, which then acts as a giant reservoir of about ten square miles, known as The Washland, The Hundred Foot Washes, or – with all the admirable directness of seventeenth-century English – The Receptacle.

Here, on a gargantuan scale, was the solution to the flooding of some 300,000 acres of fen and is the key to the artificiality of this whole part of England. But here also is the paradox: the Washland can only be used as summer grazing; it is not arable land; the peat here has remained at full depth, protected by lush grasses; this most critically artificial of places is also the Fens at their most natural. The Washland is a Site of Special Scientific Interest. The Royal Society for the Protection of Birds and the Cambridgeshire and Isle of Ely Naturalists' Trust own large parts of it which they run as nature reserves. Widgeon, mallard, pintail and teal come here in large numbers and it is one of the main winter grounds for Bewick's swans, migrating from the Kara Sea on the edge of the Arctic Ocean. When the whole expanse of the Washes ices over, it is also the best place to skate in England. In the nineteenth century the great Fen champions Turkey Smart, Fish Smart and Knocker Carter were able, it is said, to 'run down' a pike under the ice, pursuing it on skates for miles, until the fish collapsed, exhausted, and the men were able to break through the ice to haul it out.

But on a summer's evening it is a wonderful, un-Fenlike oasis, the high banks of The Washland thick with a pelt of grasses and Russian comfrey that clogs your steps, and the air filled with lapwings and that ghostliest of sounds, little more than a breath, the whirring of snipe as they drum above you.

You leave the bank of the New Bedford River on Byall Fen. It is still six and a half miles to Ely Cathedral along small lanes that climb on to the low prongs of islands in the fen, first Wardy Hill and then Coveney (which means island in the bay), and then drop back down to carrot carpets, celery fields and ditches. Most of the time the cathedral tower remains in view. You can easily imagine its extraordinary effect in 'the foul and flabby quagmires' of the pre-drainage landscape, as the historian William Camden described it in 1586.

The arrival is plain: up the hill (sixty-seven feet to the top), through gradually older streets, past The Old Fire Engine House, and into the cathedral precinct, with the slightly crumpled lines of its west front facing you across the grass. It is as though the mason had followed precisely the mild wobbliness of a medieval drawing. Did they have no rulers or set squares? You have arrived in the pre-Vermuyden world.

George Mann, market gardener in the richest soil that England can provide.

Distances in miles *Chatteris to Forty Foot Drain 1.6; to Sixteen Foot Drain 1.7; to Warth's Hundred Farm 2.5; to Block Fen Sand Pits 1.6; to Mepal 3.1; to Wardy Hill 3.0; to Coveney 1.5; to Ely Cathedral 4.0.*

Map *OS 1:50,000, sheet 143, Ely, Wisbech.*

Book *H. C. Darby,* The Changing Fenland (*Cambridge University Press, 1983*) *is a wonderfully researched, beautifully illustrated and endlessly fascinating history of the Fens and their drainage over 2,000 years.*

15.

Shopping Around

Trumbull Shopping Park

CONNECTICUT

Always have a guide in the US; it's a much more foreign place than you think. In this expedition to the new heart of the New World (there are now more shopping malls in the States than either post offices or secondary schools), I was lucky enough to have with me Doug Stumpf, the immensely handsome and brilliant young editor at William Morrow, the New York publisher. He made only one condition in return for abandoning his desk: that I should describe him as 'the immensely handsome and brilliant young . . .'.

At six-thirty on a sunny spring morning I met up with Doug outside his apartment far up on the upper west side of Manhattan. His car, for the second time in two weeks, had had a window smashed in overnight, by crack addicts, he said, looking for anything they might use or sell. So it was a windy drive out into Connecticut, which was looking new and beautiful, the drifts of white and pink dogwood, the colours of ice cream, flowering among the new green of the leaves.

Past Greenwich and Stamford, in the unhurried courtesy of American traffic, we drove out to the small, middle-class dormitory town of Trumbull, and more particularly to Trumbull Shopping Park: not merely a shopping centre, more like a haven from the world.

The mall resembles an airport terminal building, a cluster of blocky, windowless shapes, covering about fifteen acres, surrounded by a fifty-five-acre sea of car-parking. The building makes no effort to be beautiful outside. The outside does not matter. This, first and last, is an interior space, a climate-controlled cocoon, where the occupants turn away from the world outside towards a neat and un-frightening vacuum, where trees are somehow persuaded to grow, where birds in bird shops sing in their cages, and where people go for long walks in the most comforting landscape they know.

In through the double doors, to the world of de-nature. It was eight o'clock in the morning, well before opening time. The mall is on two levels, connected by escalators, with a large department store at each of its three corners and about 200 boutique-style shops filling the spaces between them.

Inside the avenues of the mall, the light was neither bright nor dim, the air not cool nor warm, the fittings neither plush nor tawdry, the place neither crowded nor empty, but gently animated by the slow, plasticated pad-padding of the mall-walkers, old people in loose walking suits perambulating along the seamless tiling of the floor. The mall is unobjectionability itself, perfect pap.

Doug and I had an appointment to meet the manager of the mall who could tell us about Trumbull's role in the new phenomenon of mall-walking, but he had decided not to come for the day. We met his assistant, Ann Marie Sultzbach, and the director of security, a super-groomed ex-FBI man called William B. DiFederico, who had a moustache that stood out at an angle from his upper lip and chains hanging from his waistcoat pockets.

This was a perfect environment, he said, for those with heart or respiratory conditions. It was far better than the streets of Trumbull itself, which were impossible for peace of mind. It was safe here, and even if Trumbull wasn't exactly the most crime-ridden place in the US, there was a perceived threat. It never got too hot or cold here; it was relatively social. There weren't any ups and downs. It was more fun than the treadmill.

I thought he was joking, but no. Doug explained how the instrument of self-improvement at the moment is the high-tech treadmill, probably the purest form of walking one can imagine, walking for its own sake, the mileage clocking up on a dial in front of you, without the bother of going anywhere.

DiFederico had 235 registered mall-walkers on his books, all of whom had signed a release to say that it would not be the mall's

Walking in Trumbull Shopping Park need not involve anything unexpected, any horrible people, any change in the weather or temperature, any sense, in fact, that you have left your own sitting room, except that it's slightly bigger.

Bunny and Hank Suchenski relax at the Food Court after their daily 1–2 miles around the mall.

fault if they dropped down dead. No one yet had, but he had to be careful. DiFederico saw something beautiful in mall-walking. 'This mall has got a rhythm to it,' he said. 'You can go round and round and round. The corridors are beautiful. This is where people can get happy. Many people come to do it here every day, religiously. And if they want to do it, may God bless them.'

I approached a couple sitting down in the Food Court, eating Dunkin' Donuts. Robert and Mildred Giannini (he an ex-school principal, she an ex-lab technician) bore the safety factor in mind. They read about muggings in the papers. There was the curse of drugs on the streets. 'We are being cautious in the backs of our minds,' Robert said. The Gianninis confessed that there was no talking whatsoever during the walk itself. It was a serious four miles every day. It was a job that had to be done.

Another group was more promising – men only, chatting and giggling. And here we chanced on the hero of the Trumbull Shopping Park. Vincent Testani is famous. Articles have been written about him in newspapers. DiFederico had mentioned him. He is seventy, is a great one for the girls, still talks English with a monstrous Italian accent, despite having been here since 1937 ('because I don't pay any attention'), and walks and runs between twelve and thirteen miles every day around the mall. This was the real thing. Could I go for a walk with him around the corridors? 'Of course, of course!'

It wasn't a walk; it was an obsession. Vinnie, as he's known, skipped up the escalators in a gym instructor way and immediately homed in on the corridor walls like a cruise missile, flicking his torso in and out of every nick and identation of the shopfronts. 'You have to keep to the edge, otherwise you don't get the yardage,' he explained. Past I Can't Believe It's Yoghourt, Vinnie broke into a stiff-torsoed trot, grinning up at me to show, yes, he could trot too. Quicker and quicker, Diet Swirl, Maison du Popcorn, Vinnie's tense old little body, flicking out the familiar path.

Vincent Testani, acknowledged king of the Trumbull mall walkers.

A female missile came the other way. The two of them dodged niftily apart at the meeting only to return to the comfort of the measured wallside path. Quick, quick, he knew every tile, Denby's Tobacco Barrel, Doktor Pet, as I jogged parallel to him in the easy middle of the mall corridor, bemused by the distortions to which this man had subjected all the graces and pleasures of walking.

Quick, quick, Complete Athlete, quick Cosmetics A la Carte. Vinnie grinned as he skipped sideways, first one way, then the next, his chest held out, his arms almost motionless at his side. 'There are no holes in the path here. I cannot trip,' he explained.

Back to the escalators and down to the lower level. Fredelle, Naturalizer, Underground, every shop the same. Personally Yours, Mr Store, Body Accents, Vinnie's grin was clamped shut. 'I am going to Norwalk, Connecticut,' he said through it, 'to visit a young lady, very nice. You?' 'I must go back to Manhattan,' I said.

We reached the Food Court again. Doug had been sitting there patiently while Vinnie demonstrated his prowess to me. We thanked Vincent and his friends for their time and instruction and walked out of the place, into the slightly windy real air where a slight and real sun shone on the tarmac, and where Doug's car was waiting with its broken windows to take us back to the city.

16.

A Walk in Harris

Outer Hebrides

WESTERN ISLES

In mid-summer it is dark in the Hebrides for only a couple of hours. The daytime stretches almost to midnight and even then, throughout the night, there is always a faintly luminous patch in the southern sky. This is the place for long walks, casually taken, not hurrying for any particular destination, careless of progress, with your brain in retirement. It is the nearest thing on earth to walking in space. Everyone should try it.

If you knew nothing about Harris, that is what you would do here anyway. But there are other things one must understand before setting off too gaily into the wilderness. The whole of North Harris is owned by a Swiss family company. Most of it is a 56,000-acre deer forest in which the North Harris Estate sells both the stalking and the salmon fishing.

In the autumn of 1986 the estate, with its headquarters at Amhuinnsuidhe Castle, issued letters to the crofters on the island, instructing them to remove their sheep from the hills within a couple of weeks – pleading a decline in deer stocks and identifying overgrazing by sheep as the cause. This aroused long and deep island memories of the old struggle between the landlord and the landless. The Crofters' Union and the Nature Conservancy Council maintained that the notice given was too short, and the crofters refused to remove the sheep. The possibility arose of another crofters' war, like those in the 1880s and the 1920s when the deer forest was invaded by crofters, deer were shot and farms from which the crofters' fathers and grandfathers had been evicted were illegally reoccupied.

Now a foreign landlord once again seemed to be putting the wellbeing of his deer – and profit – before the interests of the people whose ancestors had been removed to make way for them. The reaction was so fierce that the estate climbed down and nothing has been heard of the matter since.

All this is something to bear in mind as you make your summertime walk through these hills. The estate is vast and empty; the native crofting community is squeezed in around the edges, with almost no croft bigger than ten acres or worth more than £15,000, each held on a yearly tenancy from the estate.

As you make your way into the hills of North Harris, you are putting yourself into the crofters' shoes for a while. The law of access to Scottish hills is notoriously vague. Rights of way over these vast blocks of privately owned land are not properly defined, nor made legally explicit.

There are, as in the rest of Scotland, virtually no paths marked on the map across the empty expanse of North Harris. Does this mean that you can go nowhere? Or everywhere? In theory, the answer is practically nowhere; in practice, virtually everywhere. Like the sheep, you have no rights, but there is nothing much the estate can do about it. The factors of the North Harris Estate are anxious that during the stalking season, which runs from 1 July to 15 February, walkers should keep to the bottom of the valleys to avoid disturbing stalkers or their prey. Most people will, nevertheless, go where their fancy takes them, but it is sensible – at least during the season – to ring the estate office at Ardvourlie Castle on 0859 86200 the evening

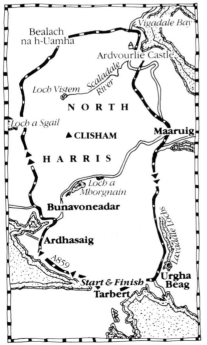

before to find out who is stalking where and to tell them of your intentions.

For the first two or three miles you follow the road west out of Tarbert, along the shores of the loch and past the abandoned lazybeds of the crofts, filled today with flag irises and reeds. Almost nobody cultivates these narrow strips of built-up soil now. The crofters were forced to create them in the nineteenth century after their eviction from the fertile lands on the west coast of Harris, which the landlords then turned into sheep farms. The impoverished soil would yield only a few oats and a bucket or two of potatoes.

Seals float out in the loch and a raven croaks on the hill beside you. Down in Loch Bun

The township of Tarbert, scattered on the hard, infertile Lewisian gneiss.

Abhainn-eadar, there are signs of one of the booming new Hebridean businesses – the netted cages of a salmon farm. In the Highlands and Islands, fish farming – salmon, trout, scallops, oysters and mussels is now worth £60 million a year. It is not a cottage industry and the five years of heavy investment before any return is seen makes it difficult, even with the grants available, for any local man to get into. These farms, which you can find in almost any sheltered loch, are subject to an exotic form of theft: a fishing boat with a vacuum pump on board comes alongside the cages at night, drops a wide hose into them and sucks out the table-ready fish, worth seven pounds each, by the thousand. One fish farmer fold me he shoots at any strange boat hovering around his cages.

Across the bay from the fish farm, in the township of Buna-voneadar, are the remains of a previous enterprise, a whaling station set up by the Norwegians before the First World War (there is the grave here of one of the Norwegians' dogs, Sam *'min trofaste hund, 1907'*). The station was taken over in 1922 by Lord Leverhulme, who owned the whole of Harris and Lewis. Whales were caught in the North Atlantic beyond St Kilda. The oil was used for soap, the meat for sausages destined for Africa. The scheme, like Leverhulme's

Distances in miles *Tarbert to Ardhasaig 2.5; to Bunavoneadar 1.7; to Loch a' Sgàil 2.5; to Bealach na h-Uamha 3.1; to Vigadale Bay 2.1; to Ardvourlie Castle 1.1; to Maaruig Road 4.0; to Urgha Beag 4.0; to Tarbert 2.0.*

Map OS *1:50,000 Sheet 14, Tarbert and Loch Seaforth.*

A landscape once populated with small crofting villages is now empty except for the occasional fisherman and a hut.

others, failed, the station closed in 1930 and now there is only the tall brick chimney from the reducing plant and a few denuded concrete floors left.

Here you climb over the fence and move on to estate land, up the banks of the Abhainn Eadar, where it is very boggy in places and the cloud is low. The sheep and the deer are further up in the mist, where there are fewer midges. On the floor of the valley it is quiet and empty, the white tufts of cotton grass growing on the wet patches, bog bean poking up in the shallow pools, waxy water lilies on others.

On the map, the names are in a scattering of Norse and Gaelic. The bigger things, the high hills – Clisham, Teilesval and Stulaval – and the valleys – Langadale, Vigadale, Scaladale – are Norse, the language of government in the Hebrides between the ninth and the thirteenth centuries. But the small places – Loch a' Sgàil, 'the windy loch', Clett nan Uan, 'the place for lambs', Coire Sgùrra-breac, 'the grey-looking corry' – are in the language the crofters still speak.

You drop to Langadale, where some abandoned houses are surrounded by pure green turf, and almost at the end of it reach the estate track created in the 1860s to connect the lodge at Ardvourlie Castle with the interior of the estate. The castle is now a hotel.

The path back to Tarbert runs across the Scaladale River and up the far side of the valley. It is an old path used, in the days before crofters had cars, by the Scaladale children on their way to school every Monday morning. They returned on Friday evening, spending the week in the Tarbert hostel. The path runs for ten miles with two long climbs. It was also the way mothers walked every week with the supplies for the family. It can't have been easy.

At the beautiful green place where the Dibidale River flows down into Loch Laxadale – the salmon valley loch – I slept for an age in the sunshine until a single brown cow, browsing in the afternoon, licked my face. It was a short walk back to Tarbert, where five gannets wheeled high in the sky, and on the edge of the town a landscape photographer sat despairingly on a roadside rock as the clouds gathered.

97

17.

Ridgeway Country

OXFORDSHIRE

Ashbury is one of those villages along the foot of the downs which mark the spring line, the point where the water which has percolated for many weeks through the chalk hills meets the layer of valley clay and is forced to the surface. The village lives on the edge of two worlds: the dry upland emptiness of the downs; and the rich clogged density of the Vale of the White Horse. You can see it in the buildings. The footings of the old cottages are of brick (baked clay) or the greenstone from the vale, but above that and nowhere better than in the long, pale ranges of Manor Farm and its outbuildings, the walls are made of chalk itself. Only the hardest chalk, called 'clunch', can be used as building stone, but even then, if you rub your hand against it, you will find it soft enough to leave your skin white and dusty.

Leave Ashbury by the road along the foot of the downs towards Wantage and after a couple of hundred yards turn up to your right past a small field of allotments and into the little branching side-valley called Kingstone Coombes. This is as beautiful a place as you will find anywhere on the chalk. The hillside is cut and folded in those half-round, half-angular, arbitrary ways that are so typical of downland, apparently as easily cut and folded as a lump of dough. Conservative cows browse under the arms of beech trees. The small buns of woodland sit neatly on the turf. There are scabious and bellflowers in the longer bits of grass, low, stemless thistles and hawkbit where it has been cropped. It is a scene of real Arcadian contentment. Nothing is sudden; everything is expected.

At the top of the hill and set a little way back from the edge is the ancient track known as the Ridgeway, which follows the crest of these downs in a continuous if slightly wobbly way for the forty-odd miles from the Vale of Pewsey in Wiltshire to the Thames at Streatley. It is so old one can't put a date to its origin but it has certainly been in some kind of use for 6,000 years. Since 1973 it has been promoted by the Countryside Commission as one of its long-distance routes (from now on to be known as National Trails) encouraging walkers and people on horses to follow the length of it.

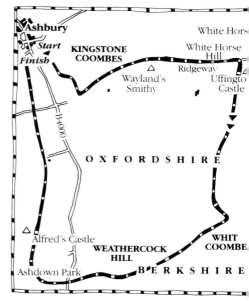

Arriving on this pedestrian motorway, perhaps the most famous walk in southern England, is something of a shock. The path itself is worn and rutted, muddy, scuffed and over-used. It is crowded with people. (Although it has commissioned a survey, the Countryside Commission does not yet know how many people use the Ridgeway. The only statistic it offers is the number of walks over two miles taken annually in the United Kingdom: 400 million. If you include 'strolls' of less than two miles, the figure is probably a billion. I can only say that on the Ridgeway, it feels like it.) The next three miles were like a drinks party. No, the Leggatt family from Six Mile Bottom, Cambridgeshire, did not like the Countryside Commission's suggestion that paths might be 'sponsored' or privatized – 'The Shell Ridgeway' or 'Debenham's Pennine Way'? Both Mr and Mrs Leggatt thought that was not right.

A few hundred yards along the track a party from Wisconsin was negotiating the appalling mud and puddles as the tour guide explained to them the virtues of a 'high dry upland route away from the mud of the valleys'. 'Really?' one of them whispered irreverently, but she was very properly ignored. They were all aged over eighty, wore identical beige trenchcoats and expensive running shoes, which were over the ankles in the mud, and were being led to the heart of England by a company called Ageaway which had provided them all with name-tags as if this were a conference. Angie, from Prairie du Chien, Wisconsin, could *not* believe that Wayland's Smithy – that beautiful long barrow surrounded by its halo of beech trees, its long turf body like a tadpole's with a flat stone head at one end – was that old. 'I cannot believe it,' she said – four times. Wayland's Smithy, a communal grave in which bodies were dismembered (a little wrinkling of Wisconsin noses here), dates from about 2800 BC.

99

RIGHT *The White Horse of Uffington, carved into the turf of the downs and regularly cleared of encroaching weeds and grass for perhaps twenty centuries.*

BELOW *The Ridgeway as it starts to climb towards Uffington Castle. This is what four-wheel drive fanatics wish to drive down.*

Angie and the other Ageaways returned to their bus. I walked on to the Iron Age fort called Uffington Castle. Beautiful women on horses with fat, shiny bottoms said 'good morning' as they passed, the bottoms wobbling and quivering into the distance.

Here the path becomes clearer and drier, the grasses and the thorn trees brush in from either side. It begins to feel – this odd, modern, linear park – something like the received image, the Edward Thomas picture of the Ridgeway, as a clear, gentle, lovely, loping thing, moving easily from one rounded knoll to another ... 'that straight line,' as he wrote, 'in which a curve is latent.'

But then, a few hundred yards short of Uffington Castle, the climax to the morning: the altercation. One of the great virtues of

the Ridgeway as an idea is that it is not an invented footpath but an ancient *road* whose legal status allows any vehicle to drive along it. There has been a wrangle about this for years, mainly on class lines. The pedestrian and equestrian middle classes don't like what they see as the loutish oiks from Swindon and Wantage driving their motorbikes and four-wheel drive vehicles through the middle of what they would like to see as the Edward Thomas National Animal-and-Vegetable-Only Reserve Parkway. The four-wheel-drivers don't like what they see as the snotty elitists trying to exclude them from a road on which they have ancient rights of access.

This drama of old England was re-enacted the other day by me, on the one side, as Edward Thomas, and by three men in wellies

The Iron Age banks of Uffington Castle, where too many people walking on the turf has started to erode it in places and the National Trust has erected hurdles to keep them away from the worn patches.

Ashdown Park, an early seventeenth-century doll's house, built from clunch, the hardest form of chalk.

and dark glasses (it was raining), three Japanese four-wheel drive khaki vehicles, chunkily designed, and three attendant, subservient women with blue eyeshadow, on the other, as the forces of darkness. It was a Sunday and I told them, I think a little airily, that there was an agreement that people like them should not bring cars like these down the Ridgeway on Sundays in the summertime. It went downhill from there. 'Why do you do it, anyway?' I asked. 'It's fun, isn't it?' the leading driver said. 'It's just another form of walking.' I laughed. More horses and bottoms squeezed past the traffic jam. Some peace people stood by, smiling sweetly in their leather jackets and long plaited hair. 'I've probably walked a damn sight more miles than you ever have,' the driver said. 'Probably.' 'How many mountains have you climbed?' he asked. I said I didn't know. 'Well, I've climbed eighty or ninety.' I didn't see the relevance. 'The relevance is, sonny, that you don't know what the fuck you're talking about.' There you go. The convoy lurched off into the worsening mud towards Avebury, past the notice board asking them not to do so, looking for the next rut out of which to dig themselves and their cars.

Goodness knows how often this scene has been repeated in the last few years. The point is that it would not happen if the Ridgeway was not promoted as the last word in downland walks.

At Uffington Castle, look at the astonishing Celtic White Horse (the oldest surviving work of art in England) and have a picnic sitting *in* the castle's ditch, but then turn off the Ridgeway. Go southwards on a high, straight path on the edge of racehorse gallops and perfect barley fields (some of the most immaculately farmed crops I have ever seen) towards the shallow scoop of Whit Coombe. It is an empty, anonymous and beautiful valley, with the path perfect underfoot, never a hint of muddiness or over-use, and a discretion and subtlety in the place which is everything you could want from a walk in England. Down in the bottom of the valley is a small, unvisited triangular wood. Go inside. There is a belt of small thorn trees, a hedge untended and grown up. Beyond them, magically, the wood opens up into a leaf-ceilinged temple, the ribs and vaults made of coppiced beeches which have not been cut for forty or fifty years. At the far end is an enclosure, in which at some time pheasant chicks were reared. It is neglected now, but still strung up on the wire fence, as an example to the others, is a line of twelve dead stoats, their shrivelled bodies hooked around short string nooses.

Beyond the wood you climb a low ridge through cornfields, with the path, when the barley is still uncut, no more than two legs wide, each ear brushing against your thighs. You come into the shaped landscape of Ashdown Park, an exquisitely pale, feminine and toy-like house, built for a seventeenth-century courtier who fell in love with a queen, never married and retired here to nurse his bachelor sorrows until he died. It is now owned by the National Trust and is open on Wednesday and Saturday afternoons in the summer.

Beyond the house is another small Iron Age fort called Alfred's Castle, again unvisited, full of docks and sorrel, perhaps the place where, in the Battle of Ashdown, Alfred defeated the Danes. It is only a couple of miles back across the fields to Ashbury. You cross the muddy and tramelled Ridgeway again. The Ageaways are still picking their way gingerly towards the bus. You reach the smooth, round-nosed edge of the downs sliding towards the vale. This is the northern edge of Wessex, the view Jude would have had as he looked towards Oxford. Ashbury church is deep in the trees. The path is lined with scabious and harebells. You will at last arrive, unspeakably content, at the Rose and Crown.

Distances in miles *Ashbury to Ridgeway 1; to Wayland's Smithy 0.6; to Uffington Castle 1.5; circuit of castle 1; to Whit Coombe Wood 2.4; to Ashdown Park 2; round trip back to Ashbury 2.5.*

Map OS *1:50,000, sheet 174, Newbury, Wantage.*

18.

Bocage and Beaches

Cotentin

NORMANDY

When Roman Polanski came to southern England to film *Tess,* he was unable to find anywhere that looked quite right. Wessex had been smartened out of existence: peasant cottages had carports, farmhouses had swimming pools. The film crew decamped across the English Channel to the Cotentin, that little stub of Normandy that sticks north into the sea, and there Polanski was able, quite effortlessly, to re-create nineteenth-century Dorset.

The Cotentin is a wonderful place for a walk, netted with an endless complex of tiny hedged fields – the *bocage* – threaded by dusty lanes and filled with cows and orchards. It is a remote and profoundly conservative part of France, famous for its cider and calvados and its extraordinarily high level of alcoholism, and for its deep indifference to events, however exciting. The Revolution virtually passed it by as another metropolitan fad and when, a few years later, Napoleon came on what was meant to be a triumphal progress through the provinces, he was welcomed by the bourgeois of Cherbourg in complete silence. It is this immovable conservatism that makes for a beautiful and quiet countryside.

Start in the little town of Ste Marie-du-Mont and straight away find the other element of the modern Cotentin: the D-day trade. This was the place where, in the middle of the night on 6 June 1944, a chaotically ill-directed parachute invasion by the American 101st Screaming Eagles dropped into occupied Europe. They were met by a division of semi-retired German soldiers stationed in the area because they were too old, too young or too exhausted for other more dynamic parts of the war zone. Most of them failed to get out of bed that morning. Others, in one terrible incident, were calmly having breakfast in the farmhouse where they were billeted when the excited and nervous American paratroops found them. They were all shot with their breakfast in front of them.

Ste Marie is resonant with the double tone of the place: a deep sense of ease and the memory of violence. The crêperie L'Estaminet,

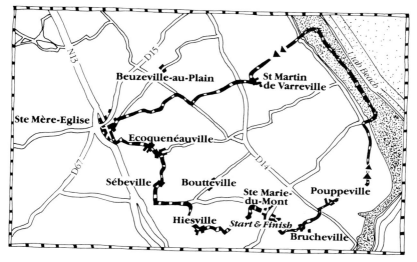

opposite the church in Ste Marie, must be the only one in France which has a comprehensive library of Second World War literature. The *patron,* Franck Méthivier, will be able to sell you guides and offer tips and hints on all the more grisly sites and events. And here, too, on the other side of the square, in a rather grotesque version of the antique shop, you will be able to buy barnacle-encrusted rifles, pieces of uniform, helmets pierced with bullet holes and other rusty souvenirs trawled from the invasion beaches or ploughed up in the fields of the *bocage*.

Leave the town square by the south-east corner and head off towards Brucheville, a mile or so away down the hill. There is a beautiful little Romanesque church, filled with semi-pagan Viking carvings of writhing sea-beasts and wedge-headed monsters. Fixed to the chancel wall is a small memorial to the civilians who died here on 6 June. They appeared at an upper-storey window of one of the houses near the church and the Americans shot them, thinking they were snipers.

To get to Utah Beach, you follow the lanes along which the parachutists moved throughout the morning of D-day, aiming to meet up with the troops who had landed on the beach itself. This was war in a picnic zone – tiny trout in the streams, a hazy, pastoral air and the ever-present, sweet-smelling cows. The Americans, most of them in small, only half-organized bands, stumbled towards objectives they only half-recognized. The party on this lane, because of the chaotic drop, consisted of two generals, three colonels, a

American tank at Utah Beach.

major, several captains and about forty soldiers and clerks. 'Never in the history of military operations,' said one of the generals, nominally in charge of 25,000 men, with whom he had no contact whatsoever, 'have so few been commanded by so many.'

At nine that morning they reached the solid stone village of Pouppeville, and for two hours there was a terrible, bloody fight from house to house, killing six Americans and nearly half the German garrison of about sixty. The rest surrendered. A tank appeared from around the corner. The Americans shot at it until a little orange recognition flag appeared from the turret. It was an American Sherman which had landed on the beach earlier that morning. By midday the parachutists and the seaborne troops had joined hands.

The lane sidles on past Pouppeville down towards the sea. A large area of the marshes is now a bird sanctuary, and on the other side are some lovely flowery water-meadows, creased with drainage ditches. You hit the dunes at the point where the Americans broke through them. There is a mass of stuff – monuments, the remains of German gun emplacements, a Musée du Débarquement and a clutter of guns, tanks and landing craft over which small boys and their fathers play at war.

Walk out on to the beach. It is huge and beautiful. At low tide, tiny figures dot its enormous dun surface. Trotting horses are raced up and down between the children on the sand. There is excellent shrimping in the tide pools. The lines of upright stakes marking the mussel and oyster beds stretch out into the almost endless shallows. Of all the invasion beaches, this was the least bloody. The German guns had been put out of action by the air and naval bombardments, and, with relatively few casualties, the Americans had soon broken through to the back of the dunes. Within a few months, forty divisions were landed on this beach, a total traffic, if one counts the wounded taken back to England, of more than a million men.

Wooded lane in the Cotentin.

Walk along the beach for about a mile and then cut inland towards the village of St Martin de Varreville, where you'll see its church on the high ground ahead of you, rising out of the coastal marshes. This, like Pouppeville, was one of the crucial exits from the beach which the paratroops had to secure. The German garrison of about 180 soldiers and artillerymen was billeted just beyond the village in a string of solid stone houses called Les Mezières, just off the road between St Martin and Reuville, and surrounded then, as now, by rough ground and some vegetable gardens. Fifteen assorted American soldiers, none of whom had even met before, were detailed to take the barracks. They were commanded by a Staff Sergeant Harrison Summers, but none of them trusted him. At the beginning they all hung back as he started to attack the buildings single-handed. Room by room, house by house, pausing now and then to regain his breath, and from time to time joined by a companion, Summers gradually worked through the garrison. In the five hours it took to move through Les Mezières, Summers himself probably killed fifty or sixty Germans, his companions, either at his side or firing from the hedges and ditches nearby, perhaps another eighty or ninety. At the end, about thirty of the Germans were allowed to surrender. When it was over, Summers sat down in the last house and said: 'I guess it's time for a smoke.' 'How do you feel?' someone asked him. 'Not very good,' he said. 'It was all kind of crazy. I'm sure I'd never do anything like that again.'

For the four miles to Ste Mère-Eglise, the market town of this little corner of the Cotentin, your way lies through the thickness of

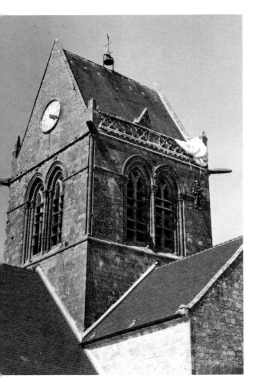

A dummy American parachutist hangs from the church tower in Ste Mère-Eglise.

Distances in miles *Ste Marie-du-Mont to Brucheville, 2.8 km; to Utah Beach, 6.8; to St Martin de Varreville, 7; to Ste Mère-Eglise, 7; to Ecoquenéauville, 2; to Sébeville, 2; to Hiesville, 4.2; to Ste Marie-du-Mont, 4.6.*

Map *Institut Géographique Nationale Série Verte (1:100,000) Sheet 6 (Caen, Cherbourg).*

the *bocage,* a defender's paradise, in which every farm was a blockhouse, every field had to be won and every hedge concealed new dangers. As the letters displayed in the museum in Ste Mère-Eglise now show, all the soldiers fighting in the area hated it. It is at times difficult to remember, but what makes the *bocage* beautiful now made it hellish then.

Ste Mère-Eglise is utterly given over to the D-day trade. It was the first town in Europe to be liberated and to that fact restaurants, cafés and the museum are all dedicated. Most macabre of all, there is a dummy of an American parachutist hitched to the church tower. Considering how many of them were shot like pigeons suspended from buildings and trees, few exploitations could be more tasteless.

The way now winds back towards Ste Marie-du-Mont through the hamlets of Ecoquenéauville, Sébeville (where you must notice the Mairie, very proper and classical but only eight feet square) and, perhaps the most charming of all, Hiesville, a cluster of fat farms around the church. Here again, although one wearies of these things, some terrible atrocities were committed in the days after the invasion.

Back through grass-lined lanes, with butterflies between the hedges, to Ste Marie-du-Mont and a bottle of cider in L'Estaminet, which you can sit drinking at an outside table while the cars stream back from Utah Beach along the Voie de la Liberté.

19.

Sunset Boulevard

Los Angeles

CALIFORNIA

When the time is right to walk across the road in Los Angeles, an illuminated sign comes on. It is not the green, sprightly, arm-swinging man you find at English crossings; nor the simple instruction – WALK – you read in other American cities; here, a rather laboured, hunched-over, wide-shouldered figure – the torso reminds one, oddly enough, of Ronald Reagan at a press conference – battles into a headwind of car exhaust and indifference. It expresses what everyone thinks about walking in LA: Don't.

But the truth is that the rhythms of this thirteen-million-people, 900-square-mile megalopolis are more perfectly suited to long walks than those of any other city on earth. 'This is the city that is relaxciting,' a woman said on the radio the week that I was there, and LA has spawned another new adjective – rurban – to describe the curious limbo in which it exists, a state of half-there urbanity, of nostalgia for an orange-grove past, of near-centrelessness, of an equivalent weight in all its parts. All of this runs against East Coast or European – or San Franciscan come to that – assumptions about what makes a city, which is in the end a sense of hierarchy, of crowning moments and subsidiary parts. LA doesn't have that and walking through this new kind of city, with its low densities and lack of climax, is curiously like walking through an exceptionally interesting version of countryside, like a *paysage accidenté,* a landscape with incidents. 'The whole place,' Alistair Cooke has written grandly about LA, 'is blanketed in anonymity.' But that is pure snobbishness. In fact, precisely *because* there is no commanding public structure, because it is a place that has agglomerated from many centres and not expanded from a dominant core, LA is one of the most self-revealing cities there is. Everywhere is somewhere there.

Sunset Boulevard flickers for twenty-six miles through these half-connected bits of semi-urban semi-city; each of them flashes its different identity at you as you pass. It's a day and a half of pure delight, ending with a bottle of Corona at the beach, climaxing in

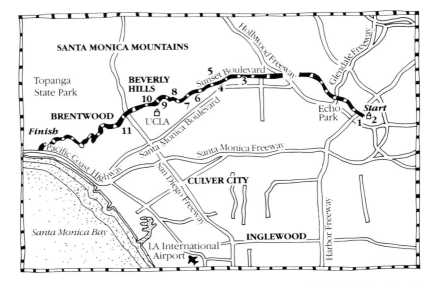

Eggs Benedict in the Polo Lounge of the Beverly Hills Hotel and beginning with an attempt at lunch in the Union Station buffet 1 (see map above). I queued there in the cedarwood halls of the 1930s half-Spanish colonial, half-moderne building, where at one time five trains a day from Chicago poured out their northern health- and wealth-seeking passengers into the Californian sun. It's a more faded place now. 'Excuse me,' I said to the four people standing behind the counter, 'I wonder if I could have a tuna fish sandwich?' Nothing happened. Entire parties of schoolgirls from Idaho were attended to while I watched my sandwich curling behind glass in the cool cabinet. I smiled. The people behind the counter looked at me as though I were a Speak-Your-Weight machine. I was not doing this right; local conditions demanded something different. Think marital row. 'Hey,' I shouted; the entire place looked up. 'GET ME A TUNA MELT.' It was there within the minute.

Just across the road is the site of the very beginning of Los Angeles, where in September 1781 the Pueblo was founded with eleven pioneer families, of whom three were at least partly Spanish, two black, two mulatto and four Indian. From the start Los Angeles had a heavy racial mix. The site of the Pueblo 2, very little of which is in fact older than the 1920s, is now a state historical park and full of Mexicans selling souvenirs. It is not a tidy sight and there is a row going on about it. The Anglo administrators of the park want the Mexicans cleared out and the whole place turned into a historical museum; the Latinos say history is people not bricks.

Sunset Boulevard begins the far side of the Pueblo. Chinatown stretches to the north of it and for the first mile or so, the boulevard is lined with a mixture of Latino and Chinese shops: Chinese funeral parlours and Salvadorean boutiques where plaster statues of Christ wearing the crown of thorns stand large and bloody for $1,200 dollars in the window; newsagents where not a single English language paper is on sale; unidentifiable parts of food. One restaurant advertises its menu as 'Thai-Mex.'

Going west is going soft. The hard and difficult parts of the city, where turf-wars between rival drug gangs killed more than 500 people last year, lie to the east and south of the pueblo. Sunset is an escalator westwards into the upscale world. I passed a braless, T-shirted whore trying to hitch a lift that way too. No one was stopping. A man in complete army fatigues and helmet, but no gun, stopped for a chat with me. No, I didn't know that Hitler had been a leading member of the Surrealist Group in Zurich in the late twenties. Nor that the Führer was exhibiting regularly nowadays in Buenos Aires under the name of Raimondo Tedeschi. Nor, in fact, now that he came to mention it, that helmets were necessary pedestrian gear in today's world, given the State of Society. I said I was happy enough to go naked into the sunset.

As the Boulevard slides on, through the scurf of cheap stores, tyre shops, insurance agents, family foot specialists and unpainted homes, the first signs of the west start to appear. In Echo Park and then Silver Lake, where the more trendy of the moneyed radicals from Santa Monica have started to move in, enjoying the street-real but not very threatening sensations of Latino Los Angeles, the first cappuccino floats up. You can see the sort of people involved lunching happily in the Sea Food Bay restaurant on Sunset and Sanborn, discussing the prospects of hiring another lobbyist for the Los Angeles school system in Sacramento and the hopes and fears for the political future in Managua. Complete and balanced pet food is on sale in Tiffany's pet store, 'pet nutrition as nature intended'.

The Hollywood sign appears between the buildings on the hills far to the west. Cast-off 1950s furniture, the same as was on sale for nothing several blocks eastwards, here drifts up, expensively, into the sub-art category in a shop called Warp. It's not what it is; it's what you think it is.

Beyond Hillhurst, Sunset dives through a section entirely dominated by hospitals and immediately beyond that arrives at one of the most enjoyable moments of the afternoon. The Church of Scientology, at 4810 Sunset, will take you in, provide you with a table and chair and ask you to fill in a questionnaire about your soul. It's all to do with goals in life, with the degree to which you are nice to other people and whether you dominate social situations. It is in fact confession by questionnaire, with no embarrassment and no unnecessary remarks from the confessor. I happily portrayed myself as one of the most exquisite souls ever to have walked the planet. But that's when the problem arose. What was I actually doing in Los Angeles? I told the receptionist I was walking the length of Sunset. He disappeared for a few minutes and returned with a man in uniform wearing a pistol on his hip. 'We would like to ask you a few questions.' I was taken around the corner. 'We do get a few spooks here,' the guard said. I understood the problem. Why didn't I take the bus? Where was I actually from? Why wasn't I hiking a regular trail? I of course wanted to be arrested for committing this most famous of Angeleno crimes – spurning the internal combustion engine – but the guard was all too reasonable. This, in the city that was practising McCarthyism even before it received its name, where young Saudi princes have been driven out of town for displaying *flesh-coloured* nude statues in their Beverly Hills gardens, was a sign that things are changing in LA. The new trend, the ultimate in its way of all trends, is ordinary niceness. No one does self-corrupting things any more; wine hardly features in restaurants, nobody knows what drugs are, cigarettes might as well have gone out with Sir Walter Ralegh. Or at least that's what they claim.

Ever westwards, on towards the glamour-zone, I ignored the Self-Realization Fellowship, the bikini dancers at the Cameo on Normandie – it was, after all, not yet four-thirty in the afternoon – and the woman who said there was a brown tide coming from the south ('It's a four-hour drive from the border'), past the chic matt modernist lines of Hollywood High and in towards the heart of Hollywood, where second-hand, swept-finned, shiny-skinned Cadillacs are for sale in fenced-off lots and where on the street you can see the wheel-nuts shaking loose with every throb of the dub dub dub coming from inside the black windows of the black muscle-bound Mustangs at the lights. In Danny's Hollywood Diner at La Brea 3, the very corner where Charlie Chaplin once made his films, gas-filled balloons float from the ceiling and you can select your songs from the table-side Seeburg Wall-o-Matic 'Is that a Cincinnati accent?' the waitress asks. No, English. 'Oh, really,' she says, 'I could never have guessed,' and you know you've been duped again.

The street scene begins to hang more tightly as night comes on.

Don't miss breakfast here in the Polo Lounge of the Beverley Hills Hotel. If you have the gall to enter with your walking boots on, remember at least to bring both the mistress and the mobile phone.

The dark fills the gaps which Los Angeles leaves for itself. The style density thickens: Chalet Gourmet, Flowers by Dolores; the Directors' Guild of America, polished granite and copper glass; Sunset Car Wash, looking like a restaurant, the Laugh Factory like a mission. A shop encrusted in papier mâché flamingos floats by; a Marlboro Man sixty feet tall stands below the Château Marmont Hotel, where Bogart met his girls. This is now the Strip, once glamorous, then rotten and degenerate, now – since the '84 Olympics – cleaned up, on its way back. There was, nevertheless, a line of customers waiting outside the Sunset Strip Tattoo Parlour.

After La Cienega 4 things start to get very smart indeed. Placards from Vogue appear in shop windows. There's a Marilyn Young Make-Up Studio. At Timothy M. Morrison some chairs are for sale with a little sign saying 'Epoque Directoire' sitting where the bottoms are eventually intended to go. But there is one sign of real money here. In North Beach Leather, a suede jacket, the colour of a cowboy's tan, the texture of a film star's skin, silk-lined, tailored to perfection, has one word in large black letters across the back. It says HOBO. A man on crutches asked me for the price of a meal. I said no. He said 'God bless you,' and we walked on in silence

The Harley-Davidson culture thickens as you move west towards the Pacific.

together past the illuminated plastic torsos holding bras, the gas braziers above the outside restaurant tables, past the car which said 'Dennis Woodruff seeks part in movie' in crude lettering on the driver's door, past Spago's, the trendiest restaurant in town, up to the right at 114 Horn 5, with no sign on the door to say what it is, but only the vision of bleached-out coolos inside, until the shame of his silence made me give him something. He then left, without a blessing this time. Wasn't it the Red Queen who screamed only *before* the pin pricked?

Just short of Doheny 6, I found my sort of motel. The Sunset-Doheny, just across the road from the Roxy, one of the meccas of the sixties music scene, feels like a survivor from the age of Sunset before the clean-up. The door to my room had a large hole cut in it through which anyone could inspect what was going on inside.

Across the road, next to the Roxy, is one of the most spectacular time-warps in the city. The Rainbow is stuck in 1973. This restaurant, called at different times the Villa Nova and the Windjammer, where Marilyn Monroe first met Joe DiMaggio on a blind date, where at table fourteen John Beluchi ate his last meal, where Sylvester Stallone, Fleetwood Mac, etc., etc. have all at different times been seen, is today filled with the most exotic menagerie of fierce female cockatoos, mini-skirted, massively haired, mascara-eyed, lycra-hugged, bra-only-beneath-leather-jacketed creatures eating onion soup and enormous pizzas as if there were no tomorrow. One or two highly manly men, in sleeveless T-shirts and chests, stand next to them, saying little, occasionally re-arranging their hair, straddling their legs ever further apart in an extraordinarily explicit display of genital confidence. One can only stand and gawp.

The next morning I set off for the coast. It was a Sunday and the Boulevard was sleepy. A few streets past Doheny, Sunset veers south-west and enters Beverly Hills. Shops drop away and you are left in the American Dream Zone. The Petit Trianon follows the Alhambra, Sansouci slots in between Malmaison and Castle Howard. Cable television fortunes emerge in the gables and granite of sub-Lutyens, surrounded by a perfection of sub-Jekyll. It is a place of hedges and privacy. Every property carries a little badge at the roadside telling you that any invasion will draw an armed response. A lady in a pink dressing gown collects the Sunday papers that have been left at her gate and returns to the purple-windowed palace of home. A Porsche or two burbles by. If you had a Martian staying the week-end, this is where you would come to show him how perfect life can be.

Breakfast in the Polo Lounge of the Beverly Hills Hotel **7**, just off Crescent Drive, cost $18.95 plus tip. An octogenarian on a mobile phone was discussing a property development in Palm Springs with his lawyer while his mistress – no, perhaps it was his daughter – sat silently in Italian silk on the other side of the table sipping orange.

Sunset through Beverly Hills is a winding country road where the cottages cost six million dollars each. The sidewalk, where it even exists, is an overgrown jungle of trailing creepers, through which you have to pick your way as if along an abandoned railway line. A Mexican-style party was being arranged in the garden of a Queen Anne house and wobbling piles of fringed sombreros lay stacked on the perfect lawns. Next door a servant was manœuvring the Mercedes convertible into the garage between the Porsche 911 and the shopping safari Jeep. No. 10000 Sunset, just west of Ladera Drive **8**, is a house called Haderway Hall (Hathaway? We had-a-way of getting this rich? I had-her-my-way? No; it is a version of the 'Er Indoors joke: She had her way in making the house as fantastic as it now is.) Her dream is a cream-coloured sub-Palladian bit of expensive trash. On the scoop of lawn outside the house is a series of strikingly realistic bronze statues. A man lies asleep on a bench, two workmen paint the estate wall, a security guard stands next to the gate and two tourists gaze in towards the dream of Haderway, goggling at the riches. This is Beverly Hills made explicit. Simply to have had her way is not enough; one of the real delights in the world of flowering lawns is that other people are not allowed to join you there. The high wall, the sleeping hobo, the gawping tourists, the security guard, the workmen making your world even more perfect – this, collectively, is a monument to the pleasures of exclusion.

A charming woman sells Star Maps on the corner of Mapleton 9. Elvis always used to wave at her as he drove by. Now, throughout the conversation, her eyes slew sideways with the passing cars, looking for stars. We talked about Mr Spelling's new place. Was it 53,000 square feet of home that the producer of 'Dynasty' had made for himself? Three football fields of residence? That's what she had heard. 'But,' she went on, loyal to the heroes in whose world she was camped, 'you cannot judge by appearances alone.'

On past the entrance to Bel Air Country Club 10, along the back of UCLA, I met a fellow walker, just out for a stroll. He told me something interesting. Whenever an unidentified body is found in the city a post-mortem is performed on it. One clue is always more helpful than any other. If the lungs are clean, the dead person only recently arrived in Los Angeles; if they are clogged with the residues from car exhausts, they are almost certain to be a resident of the city.

One of the bronzes outside Haderway Hall at 10000 Sunset.

You cross the San Diego Freeway into Brentwood and the absolute acme of money is passed. Here it is comfort, not elysium. At Barrington 11, there are, after many miles, some shops and cafés. A group of girls was saying goodbye to a fifteen-year-old boy. 'I wanted to say something to you,' a girl shouts across the mini-shopping plaza. 'Yeah?' he says hopelessly innocent. 'Goodbye,' she says, and the girls titter. 'And one other thing,' she shouts. 'Yeah?' 'You're in des-

Sunset on Sunset, where the Boulevard meets the Pacific Coast Highway and the sun drops under the Santa Monica Mountains.

perate need of some shampoo.' The girls collapse with delight and the boy touches his hair as he walks away, brushing it back up.

It's a long afternoon slide to the ocean, as Sunset curls to and fro in the foothills of the Santa Monica Mountains, the lung of open ground which separates the main body of Los Angeles from the San Fernando Valley to the north. There was a suggestion at one time that they should all be tarmacked so that the rain that fell on them could be channelled into reservoirs, but no one would think of saying that today. For all the dangers of bushfires which their coating of dry chaparral represents, and its threat to expensive homes, Los Angeles is happy to have at least one part of its area untouched.

At last between the lots you see the ocean, speckled with yachts, blue into the distance. Slowly you head for the end, snaking down the side of the hills towards the coast. One might hope for some glamorous conclusion, where at the meeting of Sunset Boulevard and the Pacific Coast Highway, two of the most beautifully named streets in the world, Los Angeles lived up to its setting. Sadly not. The junction is framed by gas stations and the traffic is intense. At the beachside, Gladstone's 4 Fish has food and beer; below you the little waves of the Pacific patter on to the beach. It's as inconclusive, as comfortably undramatic, as the city you have crossed.

20.

The Ripper Tour

East End, London

PROLOGUE
Whitechapel Road, E1

A little sheepishly, the trainee Ripperologists gather outside White-chapel Tube station in the East End of London. There are about forty of them, some with their families, many from abroad.

It is an autumn evening. One wino lies half-collapsed in a doorway next to them, his crutches stuck up into his armpits and his chin on his chest. Another, a small Scotsman, stands beside the group muttering obscenities and claiming that Ripper tourists are disgusting. He says a homeless old man had his throat cut last week round the corner in Fulbourne Street and was left bleeding on the pavement, and 'none of that lot would have given a toss about him'. He is ignored and the tour stands quietly talking in groups. Some are discussing video nasties as the street rubbish blows disconcertingly around their feet.

ACT ONE
Whitechapel Road, E1

The guide arrives. He is Michael Lermer, a tall and bony figure in his early thirties, wearing a dark suit, a tightly-knotted bow tie, gold-rimmed spectacles and carrying a small, brown briefcase. He is precise in every word and movement and might be a lawyer or a surgeon. In fact, he used to work in the Department of Transport. Someone in the crowd jokes that he was probably the man who calculated the likely volume of traffic on the M25. If he hears it, he affects not to and busies himself liaising with the TV crew and then collecting the tour fees from the group.

In the first of many such scenes, he gathers the crowd around him and begins to talk. It is almost exactly one hundred years since an 'atmosphere of terror' gripped this London slum. Between late August and early November 1888, five prostitutes were ritualistically murdered within a mile of where the tourists are now standing.

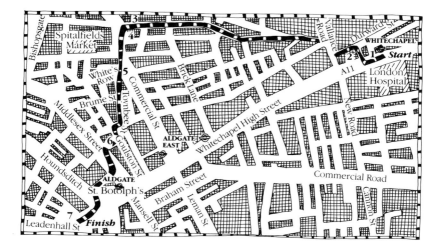

1 WOOD'S BUILDINGS *Ripper meets Mary Ann Nichols on August 30.*

2 DURWARD STREET *Body of Mary Ann Nichols (victim one) found on August 30.*

3 HANBURY STREET *Body of Annie Chapman (victim two) found on September 8.*

4 THE TEN BELLS, SPITALFIELDS *Where Elizabeth Stride (victim three) drank the evening before her body was discovered on September 30.*

5 WHITE'S ROW *Nearest street to Dorset Street (now demolished) where body of Marie Kelly (victim five) was found on November 9.*

6 GOULSTON STREET *Bloodstained part of apron belonging to Catherine Eddowes (victim four) and anti-semitic graffiti in doorway found here on September 30.*

7 MITRE SQUARE *Body of Catherine Eddowes (victim four) found on September 30.*

The murders were committed in a 'most sadistic manner'. One or two in the group titter. He quotes the cries of the newsboys, 'Murder, another horrible murder, murder, mutilation,' which followed each of the deaths.

On the far side of the road the guide points out the London Hospital, where the skeleton of the Elephant Man is still housed and where, in October 1888, the killer sent a particularly gruesome parcel containing half a gin-soaked kidney and one inch of the renal artery belonging to Catherine Eddowes, then his latest victim. Enclosed with the kidney was a letter from the Ripper describing how he had fried and eaten the other half.

The guide explains the workings of the human innards and then leads the party off to an alleyway called Wood's Buildings.

ACT TWO
Scene One: Wood's Buildings, E1

The alley is dark and narrow. It smells of excrement and urine. One tour member, a professor of Visual Perception at the University of British Columbia in Vancouver, wearing a blue neckerchief and a cowboy hat, talks wittily about the atmosphere of Victorian London. A fat woman from a small town in Indiana talks about 'messing your own backyard'. The guide, with a preoccupied and rather distant air, describes the 1880s slum of which this was a part, the 30,000 homeless people living on the street, the 130,000 in common lodging houses, the 80,000 prostitutes of a particularly wretched kind, all inhabiting the world described by Jack London in *Children of the Abyss*.

No one asks questions. In this alley the Ripper met his first victim, Mary Ann Nichols, known as Polly, a prostitute in her forties but who looked twenty years older. He led her away from the busy Whitechapel Road and over a bridge to Durward Street.

Scene Two: Durward Street, E1

The wreck of east London in the dusk. A giant, burnt-out Victorian warehouse has buddleia growing out of its cornices. Broken cars and trucks are piled high behind corrugated iron fencing on demolished lots. To the west, the offices in the City skyscrapers are still lit.

One end of the street is bright with the BBC's lights. (No Ripper tour in the last three months has been unaccompanied by press or television of some kind.) 'Is this a media event?' asks a Bengali man from a small clothes factory round the corner. 'Breakfast Time,' one of the BBC people says without elaboration, and the man nods.

The guide gathers the people under the lights, and in an effective, police-surgeon way, describes the state of the 'not particularly successful' prostitute Mary Ann Nichols when found here at three o'clock in the morning on 30 August 1888. The neck was virtually severed; she had been disembowelled and the intestines laid out on the pavement. The crowd looks on gormlessly, the BBC soundman says he hasn't been 'solid' all the way through and the guide is forced to go through his piece again. The crowd gathers willingly to listen to what they have heard once before.

ACT THREE
Hanbury Street, E1

The party has now walked a mile or so. The TV crew is sweating with the effort of carrying its equipment. Some of the tourists also look tired but they have started to be friendly to each other.

They have latched on to the most obvious topic: Murders I Have Known. There was the Baptist preacher in Indiana who shot his father; and the woman who was made drunk and pushed off a bridge by her husband's mistress near Preston; and the wife somewhere in the west of England who got her husband dead drunk and then ran him over repeatedly in their drive, back and forth, first gear and reverse, until she was sure he was dead. Then she hanged herself. The people from outside Belfast are noticeably quiet. A tone of acceptance is in the air.

The Ripper's second victim, Annie Chapman, was found at 29 Hanbury Street, now Truman's Brewery, just off Brick Lane, and almost opposite a Bangladeshi Tandoori place. She was found at five forty-five in the morning on 8 September. Her womb had been cut out, her stomach torn open and the intestines flipped over her left shoulder.

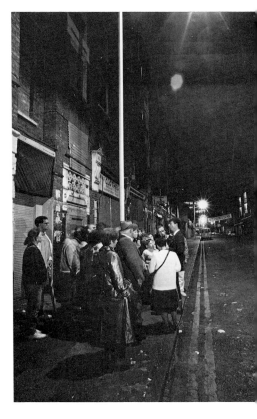

The tour gathers in Spitalfields to hear another batch of gruesome details.

To prepare his audience, the guide warns that, by comparison with the Ripper's later murders, the first two are fairly mild. He leads the party off to the pub.

ACT FOUR
The Ten Bells, Spitalfields, E1

The Victorian pub, still encrusted with 1880s glazed tiles and now full of Ripperabilia, in which the third victim, Elizabeth Stride, was drinking before being found dead, warm and still bleeding at one o'clock in the morning on 30 September in Berners Street. (Elizabeth Stride's murder site is the only one not included in the performance: it is now Henriques Street E1, off Commercial Road.)

The BBC has turned the pub into a studio with intolerable light-

The professor of Visual Perception enjoys a drink in the Ten Bells pub (above left), while the tour guide, Michael Lermer, checks some details in Wilkes Street (above right). The pub was formerly called the Jack the Ripper, but feminist pressure has forced the brewery to revert to the 1880s name. The sign now stands above the bar.

ing. The crew interviews the tourists and the guide, who in his best coroner tones tells the camera that this is 'an aspect of London's history that has to be told, people just want to know more'.

Interviewer: 'Is there a lot of money in it?'

Guide (looking at floor, smiling): 'No, not really.'

To one side, the landlady explains her predicament *sotto voce*. Until earlier that year the pub had been called the Jack the Ripper. Just before Christmas 1987, feminists had demonstrated outside, claiming it was making money out of brutality to women. Truman's, which owns the pub, didn't want any fuss and, despite the feelings of the landlady, decided it should revert to the name it had at the time of the murders, The Ten Bells. She was advised, too, not to continue selling her own invented cocktail, the Ripper Tipple. She has complied with this but still sells something called the Tipper Ripple.

ACT FIVE
(*fast, detailed and kalaedoscopic*)
Scene One: White's Row, E1

Between a multi-storey car park and a wholesale baby and children's wear shop, the guide describes the body of Marie Kelly, who was victim five.

This is the nearest one can now get to where she was found early on 9 November 1888 in Dorset Street, which has been demolished. The description is too horrible to repeat.

Scene Two: Goulston St, E1

Nothing in this short scene but a bit of bloodstained apron belonging to Catherine Eddowes, victim four, and an anti-semitic slogan: 'The Juwes (*sic*) are the men that will not be blamed for nothing' written on a door. The crowd is a little dazed.

Scene Three: Mitre Square, EC3

The last section of the walk, Catherine Eddowes's murder, and another unspeakable description, involving the arrangement of dismembered parts. It is difficult to understand why the audience is not sickened.

Scene Four: By St Botolph's Church, EC3

The dénouement: the clues dropped by the guide throughout the performance are now gathered into an answer to the identity of Jack the Ripper.

That conclusion will not be revealed here, but it can at least be said that it involves Walter Sickert; Lord Salisbury; a relative of Queen Victoria; blackmail; the Freemasons; bloodstained carriages; mistaken identities; a man called Sir William Gull; ancient ritual and what can only be described as intestinal logic.

To general surprise and delight, a small Irish woman tells the guide that this has been the most important day of her life in the last thirty years, and with that the company disperses. On the way to Aldgate tube station, the Canadian professor of Visual Perception says that this is just what he travels for: the stories that one hears.

There are several companies offering Ripper walks, including City Walks of London (071-937 4281), Historical Walks of London (081-668 4019), Perfect London Walks (071-435 6413), and Streets of London (081-346 9255), who organized the walk described above. The Streets of London walk is about 3.5 miles long and lasts for two hours.

21.

A Roman Road

The Peddar's Way

NORFOLK

If you let your eye drift over the Ordnance Survey map of north-west Norfolk to the east of King's Lynn, you will see a country of relaxed and easy lines. There is nothing sharp. Broad-backed ridges rise between gradual valleys. Grand houses and their parks are dispersed at intervals of four or five miles, a distance to suggest Jane Austenish afternoon visits between significant neighbours. Many of the roads which lope across this long-limbed country have the extended, slow-curving, lines of ancient trackways, converging on villages, diverging in narrow wishbones on the tops of ridges. Without knowing it, you would guess that this is a very old landscape indeed.

But then something will stop the easy movement of your eye over the map. Strung across it, like the route of a mechanical snail, there is another sort of road, unrelated to the forms of the landscape, indifferent to the placing of villages or to any local purpose, driving rigidly north-north-west across the country for mile after mile to the sea. This is the Peddar's Way, the most walkable Roman road in England. It is visibly an alien thing, hardly used now except by walkers and the occasional tractor, nothing to do with the country it traverses. In yet another testament to the deep conservatism of land use, the modern map shows that the people of Norfolk have continued to use the country in the way they were using it before the Romans sliced their road across it.

To walk along the Peddar's Way today is to experience this rather strange and weightless separation from the country. For many miles in succession, you come across nothing at all except the efficient wheatfields of this marvellous growing-land, and the occasional patch of sugar-beet.

If you want something detailed and fascinating, then you must

Castle Acre, a medieval new town which has scarcely grown beyond a village.

stay in Castle Acre. This is an almost perfect model of a failed Norman new town. There is a ruined castle at one end, with truly spectacular ditches and banks, controlling the crossing of the little River Nar below it, where cows lounge nowadays in the water meadows and where dragonflies dance over the surface of the water. At the other end, surrounded by a parkland of huge chestnuts, are the ruins of a Cluniac priory, set up by the lords of the castle, with some beautiful and still perfectly habitable rooms in the prior's lodgings, and a fascinating series of buildings constructed over the old course of the river: stone-lined fish ponds, kitchen and communal loos, each sluiced in turn by the river. In between the two is the brick-and-flint village, its original plan as a market town still discernible, still part-surrounded by a defensive bank and with one flint town-gate still bridging the road. You must get something to eat and drink here because there is nothing else until Ringstead, seventeen miles away.

But Castle Acre is irrelevant to the true nature of the Peddar's Way, which in a sense is a sort of sublime blank. For the first few miles out of Castle Acre a modern lane follows the line of the way (you can walk in the fields alongside if you don't like the tarmac), but after the high point called Shepherd's Bush, the lane diverges to the village of Great Massingham, and you are left with the beautiful stony track, overshadowed by old oaks and so dry that in parts it is nothing but sand, like a beach. Where even no tractors use it, there is a soft skin of turf over the stony bed of the road.

At the scale of the map, the line is almost perfect, but as you walk it, the Roman road wobbles, dips and climbs in and out of shallow valleys, crosses the many lanes cutting to east and west between the villages, so that there is nothing monotonous about it. This is not a railway line. It is something made straight but worn a little ragged, an old ruler, still recognizably mathematical but now notched and battered with age and use.

There is something else very curious about the Peddar's Way. It may never have gone anywhere. There was never a Roman town or fort at its northern terminus on the coast. There might have been a ferry here across the Wash, but no Roman quays or warehouses have ever been found. Instead, there is an intriguing theory about why this road was ever built. This was the territory of the Iceni. Their queen in the mid-first century AD was Boadicea and it was here in AD 61 that the revolt began which created such havoc through the young province of Roman Britain. After the revolt was crushed, the Romans instituted a brutal police regime in the province, and

On the route of the Roman road itself: almost dead straight on the map, curving to and fro slightly on the ground.

nowhere more fiercely than in the territory of the Iceni. Many thousands were probably killed. Almost certainly this was when the Peddar's Way was built, not as a road to go anywhere, but like a sword cut across the face of the Iceni lands, as an access route for the Roman policing forces. From any point they could move out into the dangerous territory on either side.

It may have had a propaganda purpose, too. The Romans, at great expense, built new towns such as St Albans or Chichester partly to show the Britons how splendid the imperial civilization was. It may be that the Peddar's Way, in its amazingly precise imposition on the landscape, was also conceived as a visible, tangible show of cultural superiority. What you are walking along is a demonstration of the Roman imperial idea.

Now as you pass a rare farmhouse, or the Paradise Dogotel on the King's Lynn-Fakenham Road, or the wonderful Bronze Age tumulus in a field south of Anmer, hairy with sorrel and grasses, the Way is a marginal thing. 'Peddar's' is probably a corruption of 'pedlars', those landless, shiftless people on the edge of a rural society, not travelling the usual routes between village and village but living and moving apart from the people to whom they sold their tools and trinkets.

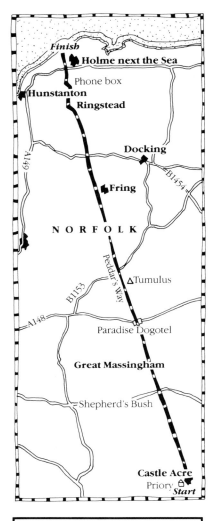

Finish
Holme next the Sea
Phone box
Hunstanton
Ringstead
A149
Docking
B1454
Fring
N O R F O L K
Peddar's Way
△Tumulus
B1153
A148
Paradise Dogotel
Great Massingham
Shepherd's Bush
Castle Acre
Priory ᴥ
Start

Distances in miles *Castle Acre to Shepherd's Bush 3.3; to A148 3.7; to B1153 2.7; to lane to Fring 3.9; to Ringstead 4; to Holme next the Sea 2.2; to the sea 1.2 (and to Hunstanton 3.5).*

Map os *1:50,000, sheet 132, North West Norfolk.*

That, anyway, is what the old road feels like today, a sort of secret route, with its own hidden purposes. You slide past the tall sails of Bircham Mill on the lower ground to the east, within a few hundred yards of the village of Fring, and then on towards Ringstead, which by chance alone lies on the route. The muddled geology of the area comes out in the buildings: every wall is a pudding mixture of ginger sandstone, brick, flint and little nodules of a sort of chalk called clunch, just hard enough to use as a building stone and which comes off dusty on the fingers if you rub it. Look out, too, in the walls of some of the cottages for that pretty building habit called galleting – tiny chips of stone pushed into the mortar between courses so that the face of the building looks as if it is covered in raisins. There is a pub here, the Gin Trap, which is apparently a traditional place for exhausted walkers on the Way to collapse into a pint and call it a day. But you will want to go on to the sea. A holiday air starts to take over. At Holme next the Sea, you find teenagers with Hawaiian shorts, then a golf course, then the dunes (there's a bird reserve to the east), and then the enormous width of North Sea sands, with family groups encamped all over them.

22.

A Promenade through Paris

St Germain to the Bastille

You may think that to take all day to walk three miles is not quite right. But this is a new style of journey – the sedentary walk.

Begin – standing – in the rue de Verneuil **1** (see map p. 136), on the very eastern edge of the seventh arrondissement. This beautiful part of the Left Bank – long, pale, shuttered streets, some of the houses with statues in their façades, the classical gateways into hidden courtyards blocked with large, dark doors – used to be occupied by the grandest of aristocrats. Look up at the first-floor windows and you will see the gilt and chandeliers of the most elegant salons. But all the duchesses have left now – it's far too expensive – and their places taken by advertising men and the refined sellers of overpriced antiques. Only at the eastern end of the rue de Verneuil are things slightly different. On one side of the street lives an English poet, Stephen Romer, in a flat furnished only with the best of European literature, paintings from the Tuscan Renaissance (in reproduction) and a mirror next to a window, via which he can see the sky. I did this walk with Stephen and these places are some of the key points in his Paris, where he has lived for many years. It could not have been done without him.

On the other side of the street, in rather more worldly style, lives Serge Gainsbourg, the singer – with Jane Birkin – of '*Je t'aime, moi non plus*' and, despite appearing in advertisements on the Métro for large department stores, the most famous existential hero in Paris. The whole side of his house is covered in the graffiti of adulation. It is the most literate spray-paint in the world: '*Ici cogite une âme slave,*' on one panel, remembering Baudelaire. Next to the door, Apollinaire: '*et tu bois cet alcool/brûlant comme ta vie/ta vie que tu bois/ comme une eau de vie.*' On the other jamb, messages of love for his daughter Charlotte from Geraldine and Isabelle with '*Bises Tendres*'. One or two adulators wait for the well-worn figure to emerge. When he appears, in denim head to foot, he smiles across the street before stepping into the waiting taxi.

Down the rue Jacob, past its beautiful children's clothes shops, its weird Historical Medical Instruments Shop, including, grotesquely, the skeleton of a human foetus aborted in the 1850s and a mid-eighteenth-century dentist's tool kit, to the corner of the rue Bonaparte. Here you will have breakfast in the café Le Pré aux Clercs (roughly translated, the Meadow for the Intellectuals) **2** where would-be Gallimard authors read four-inch thick books (no pictures) through multi-focal glasses while smoking. This is the moment to look at everyone else and hope that they are looking at you too. They won't or, if they do, it will only be until you notice that they are, when they will immediately present their chosen profile and, for as long as they imagine that you are continuing to look at them, will examine the infinitely interesting and somehow '*populaire*' outlines of the Renault 5 parked next to the pavement. To gratify them, and to see vanity at work, you should persist with the admiring gaze until they give you the quick but definite *checking look*. Both parties will then be satisfied: they will know they are truly admirable; you will know they are not quite so cool as they like to think they are. It is a high-risk strategy to attempt oneself: you may well end up examining a large number of cars while the rest of Paris gets on with its day.

First café over, and on down the rue Jacob, past a little mansion on the right-hand side of the street, its façade almost covered by a large yew tree. This is Seuil **3**, the most prestigious of intellectual publishing houses in Paris and discretion itself: its name is nowhere to be seen. On to the next seat, La Pallette **4** in the rue de Seine. If the Pré aux Clercs was Mind, this is Art. The seats for artists are distinctly less comfortable than those for intellectuals up the road. More neckerchiefs are in evidence here, no books, no half-moon glasses and many more extraordinarily beautiful women. All around the café, above the tiles and mirrors, large paintings hang out from the walls. One depicts La Pallette's most famous waiter, who attracts custom with the well-tried technique of insulting the people at his tables on the basis of their dress, face or aesthetic instincts. Anyone rash enough to produce a drawing of their own in the café will have it snatched from his hand and held up to general ridicule. It packs them in.

On down the rue de Seine to the river, turning around the stone bulk of the Institut **5**, a beautiful, curving, domed seventeenth-century façade, in which the great minds of French civilization think. Among the latest decisions to be made here is the banning of the word '*Walkman*' as essentially un-French. One should refer to '*baladeur*' instead.

Along the quais on the south bank of the Seine, past the bouquinistes selling Joyce and Pound, cartoon porn and posters of tear-stained children, to the next seat, in l'Ecluse wine bar **6**, on the quai des Grands Augustins just before the Pont St Michel. Here the theme is the Finer Senses. It is a quiet temple to discriminating taste. The seats are plain and upright, not uncomfortable, but not distracting either from the business in hand. If you have a little cheese, brebis des pyrénées or roquefort, you must choose the right wine. Make a gaffe and the thick-lipped waiter will not

In Shakespeare & Co bookshop.

excuse it. 'Ah non . . .' he says habitually, the educative parent. 'Ça avec ça?' – the short laugh of the deeply patient – 'Ce n'est pas possible.' Then the waiting with pursed lips for a more accurate choice. Go wrong again and he will leave you to stew in your own embarrassment while attending to the more properly civilized. When at last you get it, the wine is delicious, if horribly expensive.

On eastwards down the river, you must move a little more quickly here, as this is a trammelled, tourist-ridden and tourist-distorted part of Paris. On the quai de Montebello just opposite Notre Dame is Shakespeare & Co **7**. This ramshackle bookshop is the descendant of the shop founded in 1919 (admittedly on another site) by Sylvia Beach, the friend, patron and protector of James Joyce and the first publisher of *Ulysses*. As a lesson to every other publisher in the world, she gave Joyce, who was desperately poor at the time, a

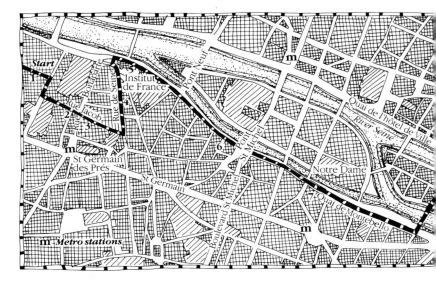

royalty of sixty-six per cent of net profits. The shop is now filled with English and American people who have that fact in mind. Most of them appear to be buying copies of *Down and Out in Paris and London*. Others come here for a free read – sadly no seats; you have to prop yourself up against the wall. If you are an impoverished poet you can ask to stay the night here in return for helping sell more copies of Orwell the following day.

Now cross the river to the Ile St Louis, turn right down the rue St-Louis-en-l'Ile and almost immediately on your right go and sit down in Bertillon **8**. It is a famous ice-cream shop with nice, squashy seats. The waitresses are surly but the ice cream is good, particularly the chocolate and the pomme-vert. This is the temple to the Grosser Senses.

If you are here at a weekend between April and the end of October, you should visit the Hôtel Lauzun **9** on the quai d'Anjou at the north-eastern corner of the island. Its vastly sumptuous rooms were decorated in the seventeenth century by a team of painters, plasterers, carvers and mirror-makers who left no space empty and no surface plain. These rooms are, in their way, a little model of the civilized density of Paris. Nothing is carefree or unworked-out; everything is almost obsessively rich and removed from nature. This is a style without ease, the decor of rigid and expensive *politesse*. Baudelaire took a room for a while in this house, but it was of the poorer sort and not on show.

On now towards the end and the highpoint of the walk. Up the Boulevard Henri IV towards the Bastille, where the new office-block-style Opéra **10** stands, a sterile thing. Skirt round the Place de la Bastille (don't try going through the Métro) and take the rue de la Roquette for a couple of hundred yards until you find the rue de Lappe going off to the right. Here, about halfway along a street of a half-seedy kind, with Moroccan nightclubs and defunct chair factories, semi-rural courtyards off it, strewn with fallen leaves, is one of the most extraordinary places in Paris. You will see its large neon sign saying B A L A J O **11** in zigzag capitals stretching the full height of the building. It is a dance hall. I was there at about four o'clock on a Saturday afternoon. The Fifties rock and French accordion music comes out on to the street. Inside is a dark and glittery oasis from the Thirties. The walls are covered in a cartoon mural of the New York skyline at night, glamour itself, played over by the lights from a revolving globe suspended above the dance floor and covered in many mirrored panels on which a spotlight shines. A bra and suspender belt are pinned high up on the wall under an amber light. The band plays on a sequinned balcony and below it, crowded on to the afternoon dance-floor, are about forty couples, most of them in their fifties or older, dressed up in silk and suits, dancing seriously, intimately, erotically, delightedly. There are no young people affecting a revivalist fad. This is no revival. It has been continuously open since the Thirties and the people here resume or preserve the style of their youth: the fast girls frankly kissing their partners as they dance; the smooth men with thin moustaches and cool suits moving between the tables; the shyer women, some sitting alone and looking, others hiring the one or two professionals, neat, courteous and charming men, who accompany a new woman for each dance, after which the fee is discreetly paid. You could stay and watch this denial of time for as long as you wanted. You might even be tempted to have a dance.

23.

Testing the Party Spirit

A Weekend in the Mendips

SOMERSET

No, it did not start well. I had arrived late on Friday evening at the Star Hotel, halfway down the high street of Wells in Somerset. The party was already sitting down to dinner – twenty-odd potential ramblers out for a comfortable weekend's walking.

It was a roomful of mutual strangers and there was, it must be said, a slight edge to the sociability. But these were practised, professional, middle-aged people. I was seated between the deputy headmistress of a primary school and a lieutenant commander in the navy. They were married to each other. Such people could lubricate any occasion. *Hallo,* smiles, cheer, what's going on here then?

There were bottles of wine on the table. I have a way (this is unfortunate) of behaving too bouncily, with a sort of exaggerated J. B. Priestley bonhomie, if I don't quite know what to do. 'Have a drink!' I said gaily, taking one of the bottles in reach and distributing the wine among the glasses of strangers. A terrible silence. I smiled like a man at a border-post. A mistake had been made. These were not communal bottles. It was not a weekend party, but a collection of little private weekend parties, all of which happened to be sitting at the same table, but *each of which had its own private bottle.* I had poured away the naval commander's entire evening's wine.

Drink works wonders. 'Don't you worry, darling,' a woman with her hair frothed into candyfloss said to me. 'I'll show you what's what,' and winked. By the end of the weekend I was still wondering what that what was.

Dinner over, Phil Scriver, the chief guide for the tour company English Wanderer, whose imitation of the wide-mouthed tree frog leaves nothing to the imagination, took me aside. The faces of the party shone like lamps above their mugs of beer, bodies crammed into wooden settles. 'Our style,' Phil said, 'is underhanded sociability,' which sounded interestingly odd. 'I mean we don't stick tails on donkeys.' No? They'd had trekkers from seventeen different countries this year. Two-thirds of this lot were back for the second

The party swings along on the first morning out.

or even third time. The season had gone well and there had been only one crisis. A New York woman he was guiding around England had gone mad on the north Devon coast path and he'd had to put her into the local asylum.

I had a blurry conversation late into the night with a couple of the returnees – a salesman with an Italian chemical conglomerate, and a brewer. 'My father's dead and I managed to ship my mother off to Australia,' drifted across the bar like a loose barrage balloon.

'Look at it this way,' the salesman said. 'You think all week. You've got decisions to make. You get enough of that.'

'Stress, right?' the brewer said.

'So what we come here for,' the salesman went on, 'is *soft authority*. They do everything for you, but they don't tell you what to do. You don't have to look at a map. You don't have to think. You're in their hands.'

This was well thought-out: English Wanderer was the re-creation for middle-aged professional people of that perennial, nostalgic dream: the Nice Nanny on a Country Outing. We went to bed happy that here in the Star we were, for a short while, safe.

I have to confess to a little morning reluctance. The alcoholic intimacy of the night before ... it looked different now. Phil had told me about his love for a girl he had met on a walk but who was

Party spirit is helped along by half pints of cider at the Hunter's Arms.

now in Dallas. The expert on transactional analysis had said her life meant nothing without love. There was the candyfloss wink. How would all of this look in the muesli glare of a hotel dining-room breakfast? I stayed with breakfast television as long as I could. But, to my relief, everyone felt the same, and we huddled in our near-silent privacies, communing with the poached eggs and the papers.

It felt as if most of the weekend had already happened, but walking finally surfaced at nine fifteen (sharpish) on Saturday morning. Phil led one party, Iain Thow the other. We were to follow the same circular track around the Mendips but in opposite directions. I was with Iain. Poor man, he did his best, I stuck with the mildly subversive lot at the back of the convoy. 'I've had a pig of a week,' a woman said whose job was to teach managers how to manage. (Later on she told me that as a reporter I was 'an intervening variable in the social dynamic of the weekend'. What did this mean? It meant people behaved differently when they thought I was listening.) Further up the line, close to the ears of Iain, it was more polite. Pathside fungi were inspected with attendant seriousness; photographers consulted on f-numbers.

We came to a hedge on top of the Mendips. A jelly-roll vision of successive haunches climbed up over the stile in front of me. The last lady in the queue stood back and said to me brightly: 'I think

Lunch on the Green at Priddy, discussing relationships and walking techniques.

I'll have a comfy stop here.' This was not a phrase I had heard before, and, always game for a new experience, I sat down on the limestone turf. There was a pause, I got out a cheese bun and sat, quite comfy, expecting her to do the same, enjoying with me this little rebellion against Nanny up front. Clearing of throats. 'I don't think you quite understand,' she said. Sudden realization that she wanted to go to the loo, apologies and a hurried jump over the stile. We arrived at a pub, the Hunter's Arms, somewhere in the middle of nowhere, reputedly run by Diana Dors's brother. (The landlady, actually called Mrs Dors, is in fact the wife of the great woman's first cousin once removed.) Some people had cider. The photographer appeared and a couple were seen sidling out of shot. A mixture of understanding and excitement from the crowd. Who could blame the poor unfortunates, finding their private weekend exposed in the Sunday papers?

We passed the other lot coming in the other direction. We talked and talked our way towards picnic lunch on the green at Priddy, then more drinks at the Queen Victoria. Strangely exhausted, we staggered on to the scenic highlight of the day, Ebbor Gorge, where Iain tried to enthuse his party for the palaeolithic life which apparently existed in the limestone crevices here. 'Three hundred thousand years ago,' he went on. One of the ladies explained to me how she had a strain in her upper thigh. A little gesture with her fingers. She had forgotten to bring any Deep Heat. 'RIGHT HERE,' Iain suddenly shouted, and a small sigh of interest in the Stone Age moved through the party. It was plainly time for tea. 'But men are so rational, so *over-rational*' ... Conversation continued as if there were nothing else to do.

I abandoned the party at the tea-room in Wookey Hole, spent the rest of the afternoon in silence, nosing around the amazing caves, and walked back to Wells on my own. We had covered only ten miles all day and I felt a wreck. The others were just as bad. Many blamed the lunchtime cider. Didn't they feel as if they had been at a drinks party for twelve hours? 'Only if you usually spend half a drinks party staring at the view,' a computer manager said. I had to admit this was usually the case. As a result, dinner was muted, if by now predictably confessional.

Sunday – again very well worked out by Phil – was a softer day, out on the meadows of the Somerset Levels. The brewer stepped in cow mess but didn't complain. An incontinent farm dog joined us and wouldn't go home. Phil told a joke about the wide-mouthed tree frog. The Pound Inn at Coxley provided beer and pub games. The Levels were hazy, beautiful and calm.

A moment of unalloyed delight came late in the afternoon. The weekend we had all chosen was graded D, the easiest on offer, and now that we had completed it successfully, one of our guides said to us, confidingly, paternally: 'I think one or two of you might well be able to cope with a C.' A C involves climbing the South Downs.

There was only one crisis in the course of the day. It was towards the end, as the party was negotiating a 'kissing-gate', not far from the outskirts of Wells. I had always thought this phrase referred to the way the gate itself 'kissed' the two little arms of fence between which it opened and closed. Not at all. Kissing gates were for kissing. The lady with frothy white hair was immediately ahead of me in the queue. She went through the gate, turned round, leant her bosoms on the upper bar, closed her eyes and pushed her mouth out towards me in a fat-lipped pout, I did not behave well and gave her the most hygienic of side-by-side air-kisses. 'Pfah!' she snorted. 'That's a yuppie kiss if ever there was one. If you're going to do it, you might as well do it properly. Life's too short, Adam.' She was probably right. It's all a question of joining in....

Note English Wanderer are based at 13 Wellington Court, Spencers Wood, Reading RG7 1BN (Tel: 0734-882515).

24.

The Most Glamorous Landscape in England

Castle Howard

YORKSHIRE

This walk, through the most glamorous landscape ever designed in England, is dedicated to the spirit of Delighted Surprise. It is a feeling we all know on a rather more domestic level, from the one genuinely satisfactory Christmas present that we get each year: the expectation of ordinariness, the dulled same-again feeling, the bleary opening of the paper, the un-novel novelty; but then, the lifted eyebrows, the half-open mouth, the very thing – ah-ha! This wonderful sensation formed a large part of the ideals of the eighteenth-century school of English landscape gardeners.

They designed with this in mind, as a form of large-scale theatre which could only be appreciated by moving through it. Not the grotesque statues, or the concealed jets of water which had so entertained their ancestors when played on unsuspecting guests, but something more civilized than that – the graceful interruption, the sudden opening of something new, the delightful surprise.

When I am a millionaire, I am going to build a temple to the experience of ah-ha and delighted surprise, à la Vanbrugh, in which everything emerges around corners and from which the obvious is utterly banished.

Begin in the pre-aesthetic world, before artificial beauty invaded this gently hilly part of Yorkshire, lying between York itself and the North York Moors. Welburn is a one-street, one-garage, one-pub, no bed-and-breakfast village a mile or so north of the road from York to Scarborough. A lane drops away from the eastern end of the village street and for half a mile or so crosses ordinary ploughland, the averagely rich Yorkshire lowland loam.

Nothing here, but then, ah! – on the horizon of the ridge in front of you, something extraordinary, the tractors raking and seeding the fields around it: a black pyramid. There is nothing explained, no visual hierarchy leading up to it. It is a random remark, an eccentricity, something – and this is the critical quality in the dreamed-up landscape of Castle Howard – *unnecessary* about its presence here.

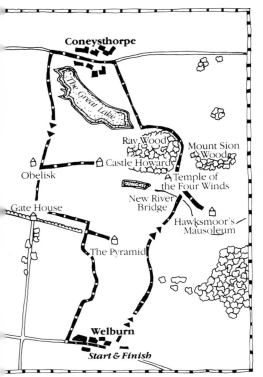

There is no great house in sight, nor any axial planning in the landscape as there would be in France. The Pyramid, sited on the crest of its ridge, is an isolated bauble, a treasured toy placed there as calmly, as apparently thoughtlessly, as a model on a drawing-room table, something taken out for a moment from a collector's cabinet of rarities and curiosities and left there while he had his lunch.

This, anyway, is the intended effect of a carefully calculated piece of landscape planning made in the first three decades of the eighteenth century by the third Earl of Carlisle, his architects Sir John Vanbrugh and Nicholas Hawksmoor, and his landscape designers, Stephen Switzer and George London.

What you are about to enter is, in fact, a staggering piece of show-off landscape. It is the most highly refined form of showing off, however, and in its way you can see it as a fossilized theatre of eighteenth-century manners. It is a display of that relaxed and enriched ease which constitutes the eighteenth-century aristocratic ideal, that politeness which goes beyond civility, in which courtesy is made to appear natural and in which the astonishing and unexpected remark, confirming the rules of civilization by breaking them slightly, is the delightfully surprising ornament on the continuous surface of life.

As you reach the top of the rise, coming level with the pyramid on your left, the Castle Howard landscape makes its first big statement. This is a rippled part of the country, in which a series of low ridges are divided by the wide, round-bottomed valleys between them. Like acts in a play, they make the perfect setting for a rolling succession of delights. Across the valley, about half a mile away, is Hawksmoor's Mausoleum, a vast, circular, Doric temple on the summit of its own hill, a tremendous, masculine thing, the unin-

Castle Howard, the garden front.

terrupted colonnade Roman in the grandeur of its severity, a temple of death.

You must cross the valley to reach it. A tall and massive bridge appears over the lake at the bottom. Giant, roughly hewn cutwaters protrude on either side. The keystones on the main arches are sculpted into masks of blind and sombre river-gods. Half the masonry is chiselled into fine architectural detail; the other half left rude and craggy, as if frost-shattered.

The Mausoleum is up to your right, beyond the fringes of Mount Sion Wood. On the other side, not seen until now, is its twin, not on the top of a hill but on the lip of a declivity, nor Doric, closed and masculine, but Ionic, decorated and open in the wide stairs that descend from the porticos on each side, and with a little windowed lantern crowning its dome: Vanbrugh's Temple of the Four Winds. It is a picnic house, built in 1724, modelled in a small way on Palladio's Rotonda outside Vicenza and standing at the end of what was the high street of Henderskelfe village before the Earl of Carlisle dispersed its inhabitants and demolished their houses.

The Temple stands at the boundary between garden and park, but sadly you cannot enter the garden from this end. The footpath, through the ridge and furrow of what had been the open fields of the village, skirts the edge of Ray Wood, originally Stephen Switzer's 'wilderness', with serpentine paths and unexpected obelisks, on the way to the estate village of Coneysthorpe. It is set around a pretty green, with late nineteenth-century Arts-and-Crafts houses and a slightly earlier model farm, now partly disused.

Beyond the village, turning the corner into the grand avenue which slices for five miles across the ridges and valleys of the Howardian Hills, you come to the biggest ah-ha of them all, the mile-long view across the Great Lake (made in the 1790s) to the dome and cupola of Castle Howard itself, a misty palace in Arcadia, its wings and courtyards spread out along the ridge, framed by woods.

And here, as you walk up the avenue to the Obelisk on the skyline in front of you, consider the validity of the idea that the human scale is all that matters in planning and design. All this is on a vastly more-than-human scale. And if anything about it had accommodated itself to the small and accessible, its meaning and delight would have been lost or damaged. Vanbrugh's Obelisk, put up in 1714 as a tribute to the Duke of Marlborough, marks the drive up to the house itself. Between April and October you can visit the house and have something to eat there. Otherwise, go on up the avenue to Vanbrugh's Pyramid Gate, set in the middle of his fake town walls, modelled on those at Chester, which for more than a mile run along this ridge, with eleven ruinous towers of different designs.

There is one more surprise before you withdraw again to the mundane. Return along the eastern limb of the town walls towards the Pyramid you first saw. Approach it quietly. Pheasants will fluster away out of the scrub in front of you and the burrs will pull at your sleeves. Pairs of strange, knobbly pedestals without statues stand at each corner of the precinct. The Pyramid is dark, its tip falling away. In the afternoon sun, the long and pointed shadow of the monument falls halfway across the earth of the ploughed field to the north. It is a haunted and unvisited place. A long marble inscription describes the reasons for its existence.

> *To thee O venerable shade*
> *Who long hast in oblivion laid*
> *This pile is here erect*
> *A tribute small for what thou'st done*
> *Deign to accept this mean return*
> *Pardon the long neglect*

It is an ancestor's shrine, put up by the third Earl to his great-great-great grandfather, Lord William Howard, who had set up this branch

Hawksmoor's mausoleum and the bridge over the lake. Nowhere else does incidental architecture achieve so heroic a scale.

of the family by marrying Dacre money. On the southern side of the Pyramid is a tiny door as if into a crypt, a soul-crypt. You enter, head bowed, and see nothing. And then, the irises contracting, you become aware of the giant presence in the Pyramid, a man, the neglected ancestor, a bust twelve feet high in the conical tomb, a boxer's head, clumsily and perhaps a little cheaply made, staring out at the sloping wall only one or two feet in front of him, dust at his feet, nothing but weeds around his tomb, the forgotten father, the most sombre ah-ha of all.

Down the hill, it is a mile or more across the rushy meadows of a small farm to Welburn village and to the shop of Mr and Mrs Smith, where at one time ten travelling biscuit salesmen used to call, but not now. They have to get their biscuits – and everything else – from a cash-and-carry in York.

Distances in miles *Welburn Post Office to New River Bridge 1.2; to Mausoleum 0.4; to Temple 0.5; to Coneysthorpe 1.2; to Obelisk 1.2; to house and back 0.8; to Pyramid Gate 0.7; to Welburn Post Office 1.5.*

Maps OS *1:25,000,* SE *66/76 (Barton-le-Willows)* and SE *67/77 (Malton and Gilling East).*

25.

Taken from the Sea

Romney Marsh

KENT

Is there anything as good as an early sunny morning in November? Nobody is awake. A blanket of cold mist sits quietly over the fields. Sun hints at you through the roof of fog. Dogs are asleep. Breakfast behind you, cold in the air. The little village of Appledore in south Kent is comfortable in its brick and tile, its weatherboarding, its heavily curtained windows, its parked cars and mown verges, its rebuilt church (rebuilt in 1380 after a French raid). You feel like a burglar in a drawing room.

But this is the edge of something different. Appledore is now eight miles from the sea, but 600 years ago the French had sailed straight up here to do their damage, coming in at high tide over the mudbanks and shoals of a huge river estuary. That salty treacherous estuary has now gone. Everything between here and Dungeness has been converted into dry land, the fine sheeplands of Romney, Denge, Walland and Guldeford Marshes, known collectively as The Marsh.

There is nothing marshy about it now; you will scarcely get your feet wet in a day's walk across it. But it is something more interesting than a simple bog. It is a late medieval landscape scattered with the evidence of its own reclamation – the banked and ditched 'innings', where part by part the archbishops of Canterbury, the temporal and spiritual landlords of the Marsh, extended their property and their diocese; the sand and sea-pebbles surfacing in the earth of those fields which are now ploughed; abandoned ports; tiny settlements each with its own church.

From the southern end of Appledore, you drop down the ancient shoreline on to the level of the Marsh. You leave old Kent for the new country of flatness, of herons, ague, eels and marshmen. Its very edge is marked now by the Royal Military Canal, a ditch seventy feet wide built between 1804 and 1809 to prevent Napoleon invading England. It was, of course, never put to the test, but it is difficult to imagine that this little weed-covered drain would have done much to deter him.

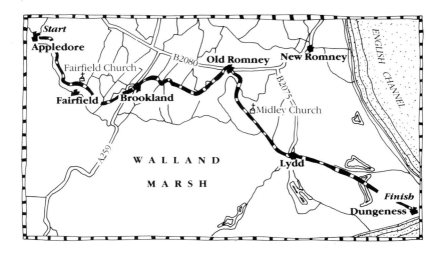

Then you are on to the marsh itself, ploughed and planted here, as fifty per cent of it now is, with huge efficient fields of winter wheat and barley. The farms are industrial and charmless, but the mist rises in plumes like taper-smoke from the ditches. Herons poke about in them and creak into flight. The lane to Fairfield wobbles to and fro along the edge of an inning made in about 1339, the medieval cuts and decisions guiding you through the fog.

But then in a marsh miracle, the mist clears and you see your way southwards across a spread of yellowing pasture, the willows stark against the southern light and, as a block of shadow in the foreground, the most photogenic of all marsh buildings, Fairfield church, set on its own in a spread of grass.

On over the pastures – there are bridges across the ditches (or 'sewers', as they are called), from which snipe burst out in a flurry of noise and wings – to come after a mile or two to Brookland. I recommend the enormous breakfast at the Laughing Frog teashop in the village. But you must not miss the church here – a crumbling chaos of different ages and styles, unperfected by the Victorians. It has various extraordinary elements to it: a Norman lead font on which – uniquely – both the signs of the zodiac and the phases of the rural year are arranged in twin arcades around the bowl; a portable shelter for eighteenth-century clergymen to prevent them from getting wet at rainy funerals; and an amazing wooden sixty-foot-high free-standing belfry, clothed in cedar shingles. It was built in wood because a tall stone bell-tower would have been too heavy for the shifting and unreliable subsoil.

St Thomas à Becket church at Fairfield.

You move on. The next church is at Old Romney, four miles away. The country in between is rougher and scraggier, the buildings a little decrepit, the landscape a little trammelled with the mess of wire and rubbish. And the same is true of Old Romney itself. The church here is dedicated to St Clement, a harbour saint who was martyred by having an anchor tied around his neck and being thrown into the sea. Now grassy and lichened outside, St Clement's has the bulky barn-like shape of so many of the marsh churches. No Victorian gentleman ever built his house down on the marsh and the church-restorers never transformed these places with their precision.

The November day already feels like evening. The light has yellowed and the high ground to the west above Rye stands out darkly in the sky. Less than two miles south of Old Romney is the ruined church of Midley. It is nothing. One holed wall on a mound that rises slightly out of a barley field. Midley means 'middle island' – in between, that is, Romney and Lydd (whose name means 'shore').

I had first thought I might end at Lydd, where the tower of All Saints stands up like a beacon above the orchards surrounding the town on the northern side. But I was there early enough to think of something more. I had – strange Sunday tea-time in an English November – a delicious curried pheasant in the Lydd Tandoori, just up the High Street from the church; and while there, looking at the map, decided to continue in the encroaching dark to the tip of Dungeness, four miles away.

It was the most magical part of the day. Leaving the neat streets of Lydd behind, the way crosses Denge Marsh, a piece of farmland as grim and impoverished as any in the south of England. The stones of the great shingle promontory of Dungeness start to appear in the hopeless fields. The farmhouses are untended, as poor now as they have ever been. This is to be endured for twenty minutes or so, and then you leave Denge Marsh for the shingle of Denge Beach itself,

Pylons stalk away from the two nuclear power stations at Dungeness.

covered with broom and strange salt plants crouching in the shingle.

Hares run out from hiding places and disappear into the scrub. Giant gravel pits are filled with blank pools of water. The dark comes on.

The two lighthouses at the far point, one dark, one lit, stand out against the last of the light in the sky. Beside them, magically orange and sulphurous in the night, a mixture of technology and palace, the most astonishing buildings in Kent, the two nuclear power stations, a radar arm revolving on the roof of one, the huge windowed spaces of their walls half-revealing the pipes and cylinders inside, steam emerging from a narrow spout at one corner, swept every ten seconds by the white lighthouse beam.

It is like nowhere else, as far removed from the Marsh as the Marsh itself is from the higher, dryer country inland. This is entirely new country. Dungeness is growing – ten feet further towards France every year.

Map OS *1:50,000, sheet 189, Ashford and Romney Marsh.*

Distances in miles *from Appledore to Fairfield 2.6; to Brookland 2.5; to Old Romney 4.2; to Midley Church 1.7; to Lydd 1.9; to Dungeness 4.1.*

Books: *The two best books are* Romney Marsh *by Walter J. C. Murray (Robert Hale, 1982) and* The Gift of the Sea – Romney Marsh *by Anne Roper (Birlings, 1984).*

26.

Through the Tops of the Clouds

Wasdale

CUMBRIA

You have left behind plum pudding, religion, the quite interesting presents, the truly appalling presents, the even more appalling attempts at pretending that appalling presents aren't that bad after all – you have abandoned all that and delivered yourself instead deep into the middle-of-winter Lake District. The air itself is a relief, a sharp draught of something fresh.

Wasdale Head is about as remote as you can get in England, the green end of a valley pushed deep between the most famous hills there are: Scafell and Scafell Pike on one side, the huge cragged triangle of Great Gable at the end and, to the north, the wide, unbroken block of Pillar. Their notched and curving horizons come halfway up the sky. At midnight the constellations are sawn in half by these hills: only the head and shoulders of Orion, no handle to the Plough.

At breakfast, with the first light, the cloud came in, sidling over the passes and across the summits, resting there like a mink collar. Scott Naylor, in whose farmhouse I was staying looked a little glum.

'I don't want to pour any cold water,' he said, 'but if the cloud's in there' – he pointed up 2,000 feet above him at the saddle between Great Gable and Kirk Fell – 'it doesn't often shift.'

Cloud or no cloud, I didn't care, I was going. What was he planning to do today? 'Oh, I'm going up there to collect some sheep.' He pointed casually at the black-shadowed mass of Yewbarrow above us as if it were a trip to the post office. I asked him if everything was all right for the farmers here nowadays?

'Everything's like it usually is. Except these nature reserves.' There are Sites of Special Scientific Interest everywhere. 'There's one over there. That's got a frog in it. One up there. That one's got a spider in it. And one up there.' He pointed towards the margins of the mist, high on the side of Great Gable. 'Got some moss in it. Can't do anything with any of them. Can't take any of that gorse out. Spoil things for the spider, wouldn't it?'

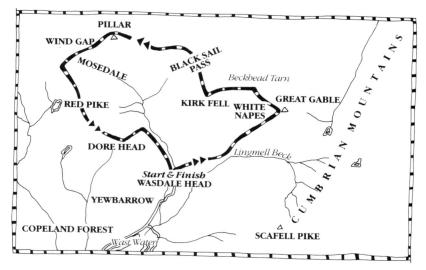

The smooth and nibbled turf of the dale floor slides up without interruption on to the lower slopes of Great Gable. The streams dropping from above after a dry year are only a thread in the furrows of their raw and broken courses. The bracken gives out and the path to the summit veers right on to the scree. The way up now for a while is scrabbling on a surface that gives and slips beneath you.

To the west, beyond the net of fields in Wasdale Head, Wast Water itself is an oarblade of slate, unruffled and unreflective. The lower reaches of the cloud come in around you as the slope steepens. No more views, just the half-dark of the mist. The grasses are stiffened by the wind-frost, each stem broadened by a quarter of an inch or more with a scimitar-blade of ice. The faces of the rocks on White Napes have a skin of ice, too. The climbing alongside them is steep now and, for all the frost, the air does not feel cold.

As you climb, the surface of the hill is always just there a foot or two in front of your nose. Keep just on the south-eastern edge of White Napes, where the mixture of rock and grass meets the scree of Little Hell Gate, which as its name suggests is not worth trying to climb. (Wainwright's guidebook, *The Western Fells,* is very useful here if you are not sure.)

The mist comes close, a quietening, muffling thing. The only sound is the cold hiss of Lingmell Beck 2,000 feet below. A sheep starts up from behind a rock and runs off to merge with the cloud. But then something miraculous begins to happen. Quite suddenly the cloud lightens. The sun can be seen through it, an exact disc the

Great Gable in the background, the intricate net of fields at Wasdale Head, and in the foreground the animals to which this entire landscape is devoted – Herdwick sheep.

size of your little fingernail. A few steps higher and the cloud pulls apart in the ragged torn way of cotton wool, strings of the two parts clinging to each other across the growing gap. Through the gap to the sudden, undiluted meridian-blue of the above-cloud sky; running up these last steps – breathless, slipping over the frosty rocks.

The view is clear to every identical white horizon. The summit of Great Gable is an island clear above this cloud-sea. Around you are the other summits, silhouetted, black, without detail: the lumpen archipelago of Great End, Scafell and Scafell Pike, the cloud nosing in at the gaps and promontories between them; the low islet of Pillar, just emerging; the spike of Helvellyn, as lonely as Rockall; and in the eastern distance the low barrier-island line of the Pennine ridge. Between them all, vast bodies of cloud, with soft and folding hollows inside them, move past at ten miles per hour, twenty miles per hour, the wind itself made visible, tidal currents of cloud, but unlike the real sea in that each part of this moving mass remains unchanged by its movement, a sea without weight or gravity. There is no chop or swell here, only the quiet flood-tide of the cloud.

And then it went. An arm of mist reached up and engulfed me. In one instant I moved from the sky-island to a winter mountain. Of course, what I hoped for now was the same thing again from the top of Pillar, three and a half miles away to the north-west. Slither down the screes in the mist to the north-west of Great Gable and pause for some soup by the dried-up Beckhead Tarn, then up to Kirk Fell, the frost blown into thick starched feathers downwind of the rocks, the buried stones hard on the feet under the skin of moss and turf. Memories of a summer walk here fifteen years ago with my shirt off in the burning sun and the fells pale and bright around me. Nothing visible now. Down to Black Sail Pass below the cloud for a moment, and a view into the dark rounded scoop of Mosedale. A raven croaks and flutters over the pass. The ridge beyond it climbs steadily to the summit of Pillar. Cairns and the remains of an old fence lead the way to the top.

I was looking as I climbed for that telltale thinning of the mist, the hint of clarity, of blue showing in the sky above. But the air stayed grey, grey, grey. Nothing, no second revelation to repeat the summit of Great Gable. I arrived at the top and sat down for more soup in the lee of a cairn. Pillar was deep in mist. There was nothing to be done about it. I closed my eyes and dozed, warm and tired, alone on top of a misty mountain.

Not for long. I looked up. Something had happened. The sky had cleared, I could see the vapour trails of two jets cut clean across it, but I and the cairn by which I was lying were still in the mist. I stood up. My feet remained foggy but my head was in the sunny air. I was standing *in the very top of the clouds.* Just below my knees the cloud began, dancing over the coarse and broken surface of Pillar. It was stage lighting, floating billows of dry ice, the low sunlight cutting through it, casting heavy exaggerated shadows from everything it touched. It was that picture by Caspar David Friedrich, the most extreme of all romantic icons, called, of course, *The Wanderer above the Sea of Mist,* but here made extraordinarily real.

I danced around half in, half out of the cloud, my huge shadow on the cloud-top weirdly haloed around with four or five concentric rainbows, my arms cutting wide spokes of shadow through them. It was an effect I have often read about but never hoped to see. This was worth abandoning Christmas for! Then it ended. The cloud folded over again and Pillar returned to the visual consistency of an old damp fleece.

I was late now. Too much romantic dancing about had left me with a long way to go before dark. But I have never had such a day, and the four miles still to be covered slipped past, over Wind Gap, around the corner of Mosedale, up and over Red Pike to the broad saddle of Dore Head. Here, for the first time since Black Sail Pass, I came below the mist. The lower half of Kirk Fell appeared in front of me, smooth and taut like the canvas slopes of a tent.

The end of the day was still 1,000 feet or so below me. Those last moments can be the most grinding part of a day's walk, the thigh-

A barren country; the view from the top of Kirk Fell.

INSET *The Wasdale Head Hotel and behind it the mass of Yewbarrow.*

tightening, knee-wrenching descent into a valley that never seems to come any closer. But from the Dore Head there is a luxurious form of descent, the nearest the natural world ever comes to a down escalator: a scree-run. For 400 or 500 feet a fine-grained tongue of fist-sized pebbles slithers you downwards in a strangely exhilarating, almost weightless way, each foot walking six or eight feet at a bound, the body tensed, the arms flung out sideways for balance. With a small bow-wave of scree up around your boots and socks, you half-ski, half-moonwalk – one of the happiest forms that walking can ever take – down towards the valley floor, where at last you arrive with a sudden end-of-travelator bump. From there on it is easy grass.

In the encroaching dark I made my way along the stream back to the Naylors in Row Head Farm. Cathy Naylor was in the kitchen. 'Good walk?' she said. 'Yes, great, thanks.' A large number of belongings were scattered over the tables. 'Are you packing to go somewhere?' I asked her. 'Yes, yes, I'm going to the Canaries. It's a sixtieth birthday present. It'll be nice to get away from here in the wintertime.'

Guide and information *A. Wainwright's* The Western Fells *(Westmorland Gazette) is by far the best walking guide to the area, particularly for the ascent of Great Gable, which can be confusing in mist. General information can be had from the Cumbrian Information Office (0966–24414).*

Equipment *For winter walking in the fells you must have all the right equipment and know how to use it. To keep you safe: maps, compass, torch and whistle. To keep you dry: waterproof trousers and jacket. To keep you warm: several layers of clothing, hat, gloves, survival bag, spare clothes, a thermos of hot soup, chocolate and other food.*

Don't do anything you suspect you can't. Tell the people you're staying with where you are going and when you expect to be back. To do this walk on a midwinter day you must leave Wasdale Head by 7.30 am.

You should be at the top of Great Gable by about 10.15 am, at Black Sail Pass by noon, Wind Gap by 1.30 pm. If you get behind, drop back down into Wasdale from Beck Head or into Mosedale either at Black Sail Pass or Wind Gap. It's much easier to get home from the valley.

Distance in miles (and altitude in feet): *Wasdale Head (240) to Great Gable (2,949) 2.2; to Beckhead Tarn (2,000) 0.6; to Kirk Fell (2,630) 0.75; to Black Sail Pass (1,800) 1.4; to Pillar (2,927) 1.4; to Wind Gap (2,550) 0.25; to Scoat Fell (2,750) 0.8; to Black Comb Head (2,500) 0.3; to Red Pike (2,700) 0.4; to Dore Head (1,600) 1.1; to Wasdale head 1.2.*

Maps OS *1:25,000:* The English Lakes, North West *and* South West *sheets. (The OS 1:50,000 or 1 in. maps are not detailed enough for proper navigation in mist.)*

Index

Page numbers in *italics* denote photographs, those in **bold** denote maps.

*There is no harbour at Dungeness; the fishing boats
are simply hauled up on to the shingle.*